A Teacher's Guide to

Writing Workshop Minilessons

Grades K–8

Lisa Eickholdt and Patricia Vitale-Reilly

Heinemann • Portsmouth, NH

Heinemann
145 Maplewood Avenue, Suite 300
Portsmouth, NH 03801
www.heinemann.com

The authors and publisher wish to thank those who have generously given permission to reprint borrowed material:

Excerpt from *A Teacher's Guide to Writing Workshop Essentials: Time, Choice, Response* by Katherine Bomer and Corrine Arens. Copyright © 2020 by Katherine Bomer and Corrine Arens. Published by Heinemann, Portsmouth, NH. Reprinted by permission of the Publisher. All rights reserved.

Excerpt from *Teaching with the Brain in Mind*, Second Edition by Eric Jensen, page 37, Figure 3.2, Alexandria, VA: ASCD. Copyright © 2005 by ASCD. Reproduced with permission. All rights reserved.

Excerpt from "Answering Your Questions About Teaching Writing: A Talk with Donald H. Graves" by Donald H. Graves. Used by permission of Scholastic Inc.

Excerpt(s) from *Last Stop on Market Street* by Matt de la Peña. Text copyright © 2015 by Matt de la Peña. Used by permission of G. P. Putnam's Sons Books for Young Readers, an imprint of Penguin Young Readers Group, a division of Penguin Random House LLC. All rights reserved.

Excerpt from *Jabari Jumps* by Gaia Cornwall. Copyright © 2017 by Gaia Cornwall. Reproduced by permission of the publisher, Candlewick Press, Somerville, MA.

Excerpt from "Transactional Heat and Light: More Explicit Literacy Learning" by Randy Bomer from *Language Arts*, Vol. 76, No. 1 (1998). Copyright © 1998 by National Council of Teachers of English. Reprinted by permission of the National Council of Teachers of English.

Library of Congress Cataloging-in-Publication Data
Names: Eickholdt, Lisa, author. | Vitale-Reilly, Patricia, author.
Title: A teacher's guide to writing workshop minilessons / Lisa Eickholdt and Patricia Vitale-Reilly.
Description: Portsmouth, NH : Heinemann, [2022] | Series: Classroom essentials | Includes bibliographical references.
Identifiers: LCCN 2021048321 | ISBN 9780325108599
Subjects: LCSH: English language—Composition and exercises—Study and teaching (Elementary). | Lesson planning. | Composition (Language arts)—Study and teaching (Elementary).
Classification: LCC LB1576 .E3495 2022 | DDC 372.6/044—dc23/eng/20211213
LC record available at https://lccn.loc.gov/2021048321

Editor: Holly Kim Price
Production: Victoria Merecki
Cover and interior designs, typesetting: Vita Lane
Photography: Elena Skinner (pages 7–10, 121); © FatCamera/Getty Images (page 77)
Videography: Sherry Day
Video editing: Paul Tomasyan
Manufacturing: Val Cooper

Printed in the United States of America on acid-free paper.
1 2 3 4 5 MPP 26 25 24 23 22 PO 34003

Book Map

Now let's look closely at *how* to teach each part of a minilesson . . .

Online Resources

To access the Online Resources for *A Teacher's Guide to Writing Workshop Minilessons*:

1. Go to http://hein.pub/Minilessons-login.
2. Log in with your username and password. If you do not already have an account with Heinemann, you will need to create an account.
3. On the Welcome page, choose "Click here to register an Online Resource."
4. Register your product by entering the code WRITEMINI (be sure to read and check the acknowledgment box under the keycode).
5. Once you have registered your product, it will appear alphabetically in your account list of My Online Resources.

Note: When returning to Heinemann.com to access your previously registered products, simply log into your Heinemann account and click on "View my registered Online Resources."

The online resources for *A Teacher's Guide to Writing Workshop Minilessons* include helpful charts and templates to use as you plan and deliver minilessons.

Online Resource 2.1	Write and Reflect Chart
Online Resource 2.2	Notice, Name, Note Chart
Online Resource 3.1	Minilesson Planning Template
Online Resource 8.1	Kidwatching Chart
Online Resource 8.2	Whole-Group Assessment Chart

You'll also find an introductory video, twelve video clips of Lisa and Patty teaching the different parts of a minilesson, and three examples of full minilessons.

Video 1.1	Welcome Reader
Video 3.1	Recap Type of Connection
Video 3.2	Tell a Story Type of Connection
Video 3.3	Metaphor Type of Connection
Video 4.1	Teacher Model
Video 4.2	Mentor Text
Video 4.3	Shared Writing
Video 4.4	Shared Inquiry
Video 5.1	Active Engagement with the Model Used in the Teaching Portion
Video 5.2	Active Engagement with Students Using Their Own Writing
Video 6.1	Example of the Link as a Reminder and Invitation
Video 6.2	Example of Link Where Teacher Asks Students to Make a Plan
Video 6.3	Example of Students Staying on the Carpet and Working with the Teacher
Video 7.1	Sample Minilesson 1
Video 7.2	Sample Minilesson 2
Video 7.3	Sample Minilesson—Asynchronous

Chapter 1

What Is a Minilesson and Why Is It Mini?

Video 1.1 Welcome Reader

THIRD-GRADE TEACHER TRACY SITS DOWN in her seat on the bench closest to the easel in the minilesson meeting area of her classroom. Her students are already seated, writer's notebooks in hand, quietly chatting. As soon as Tracy sits down, they know to turn their attention to her.

Writers, I have been so inspired by all of your thinking and writing in this argument writing unit. Yesterday when I was conferring with Emma, we were talking about the draft of her letter. She, like most of you, is so passionate about her topic—convincing the town rec center to have Friday night get-togethers for students in grades 3–5, not just students in grades 6–8. But what Emma noticed, and what she wanted help with, was capturing a specific kind of voice in her letter. In an earlier draft, Emma used phrases from her home language. She was trying to be persuasive, but not bossy; informative, but not preachy. So I taught Emma a strategy I use in my own writing—have a conversation about the topic with a partner and jot down specific words that represent you and your passion and that will achieve the effect you are going for. So today, writers, I am going to teach you how to do that—how to have conversations about your topic—with yourself or your writing partner to capture specific language and lead you to the voice you want your piece to embody.

Across town, Kristin teaches in the same district, same grade, and uses the same curriculum and curricular resource. When Kristin sat down with her students to start the same minilesson it went something like this:

Writers, my favorite show was on last night (students laugh, nod their heads, and somewhat simultaneously say, "The Voice") and I was so intrigued by the advice Kelly Clarkson was giving to a contestant. She was telling her that she was quite talented, but that she has to stop trying to be like the singers she admires. She told her that she can belt out parts, but not to try to be Lady Gaga when she did so. And she should certainly hold the notes that deserve holding, but she should not do so exactly like Taylor Swift. She told her that she has to find her own voice. That got me thinking about writing (a few giggles from the crowd). When we are writing persuasive letters, we need to make sure that we have found our voice—authoritative but not bossy, informative but not preachy. So today, writers, I am going to teach you how to do that by having conversations about your topic—conversations with yourself or your writing partner that will allow you to capture specific language and lead you to the voice you want your piece to have.

Tracy and Kristin are at the same point in their third-grade district-mandated unit of study. The district curriculum helps them know what to teach but how they bring that curriculum to life in their classroom depends on their unique style and the needs of their students. Tracy chose to use Emma's piece as an example or mentor text for how to apply a particular strategy. Kristin taught the minilesson by using her own writing as the model for that same strategy.

A Minilesson Is a Part of the Writing Workshop

A minilesson is one part of writing time, commonly known as a writing workshop, which consists of three parts: minilesson, independent writing time, and share time.

The minilesson is the time when you teach the whole class about one particular aspect of writing: process, habit, genre, craft, or convention. Tracy and Kristin were teaching students the craft of how to capture voice in their letters. We learned about minilessons many years ago from Lucy Calkins, the educator who used the term to describe whole-class gatherings. In *The Art of Teaching Writing* (1994), Calkins explains:

> *Just as the art instructor sometimes pulls students who are working at their separate places in the studio together in order to demonstrate a new technique, so too, writing teachers often gather their students for brief whole-class meetings. I call these gatherings mini-lessons. The mini-lesson can serve as a forum for planning the day's work, as a time to call writers together (like the huddle at the start of a football game), or as a time for demonstrating a new method. (193)*

MINILESSON

Students receive direct instruction from the teacher, a guest writer, or a student in some aspect of the writing process, kinds of writing, composition techniques, language skills, or materials and tools.

INDEPENDENT WRITING TIME

Students focus on their writing work and the teacher confers with individuals, partners, or small groups.

SHARE TIME

Students teach each other as they share something about their writing or their process with a partner, a small group, or the whole class.

From Bomer and Arens (2020)

Minilessons Have a Four-Part Structure

Minilessons have a frame, an organization, a way that they go. Many teachers are familiar with the four-part structure that includes connection, teaching, active engagement, and link (Anderson 2000; Calkins 1994). Embracing this predictable structure allows your teaching to be efficient, focused, engaging, and student-centered.

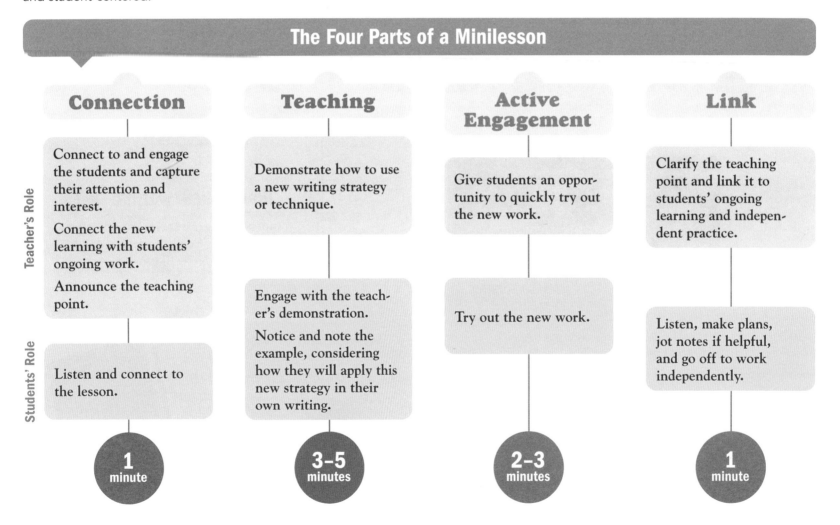

The Four Parts of a Minilesson

Teacher's Role

Connection
- Connect to and engage the students and capture their attention and interest.
- Connect the new learning with students' ongoing work.
- Announce the teaching point.

Teaching
- Demonstrate how to use a new writing strategy or technique.

Active Engagement
- Give students an opportunity to quickly try out the new work.

Link
- Clarify the teaching point and link it to students' ongoing learning and independent practice.

Students' Role

Connection
- Listen and connect to the lesson.

Teaching
- Engage with the teacher's demonstration.
- Notice and note the example, considering how they will apply this new strategy in their own writing.

Active Engagement
- Try out the new work.

Link
- Listen, make plans, jot notes if helpful, and go off to work independently.

1 minute | **3–5 minutes** | **2–3 minutes** | **1 minute**

A Minilesson Is a Culturally Responsive Teaching Move

In the opening anecdotes, we shared two examples of third-grade teachers responding to the academic and social-emotional needs of their students. A minilesson framework allows teachers to connect a lesson—often one that is mandated by a set of standards, a district curriculum, or a grade-level unit plan—to the cultural knowledge and experiences of the students.

During a minilesson, we can draw on what we know about our students and our shared experiences. The most effective minilessons will triangulate academic learning, cultural responsiveness, and the social-emotional needs of our students.

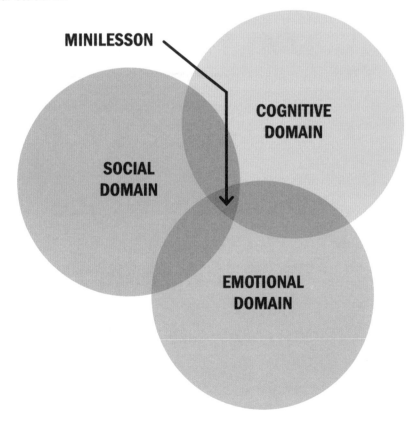

Inclusive Practices to Support Every Writer

Charts and visuals are popular tools in classrooms. Although visuals are a useful tool, they can actually detract from learning. Oftentimes visuals are overly busy with words, colors, and pictures. So, think less is more, clean rather than busy. As a general rule of thumb:

1 Use visuals that represent the array of learners in our classrooms and our world. This means including people who serve as windows and mirrors for our students.

2 When creating charts, consider adding no more than four ideas to the chart.

3 Use only phrases with carefully chosen words to depict each idea.

4 Use color to show both differences and similarities with a concept.

5 Consider, but don't feel the pressure to add, a picture/illustration.

Here's an example of a chart that lists ways students can make their story come alive:

Making Our Story Come Alive

- Describe the action

- Include dialogue

- Tell the inner thinking of the character

Where Do Minilessons Take Place *and* What Tools Do I Need?

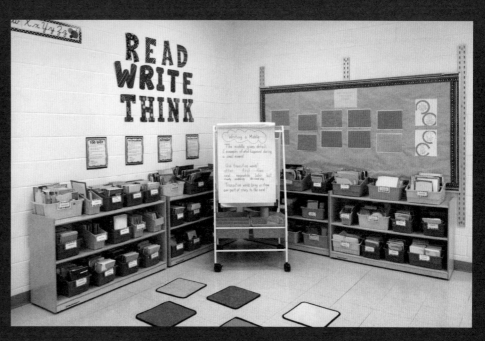

Every classroom needs a designated meeting area to conduct daily minilessons. An easel makes creating charts and demonstrating writing easier. Carpet squares allow students to create smart spots to sit and listen during the lesson.

Using bookshelves and lighting, this meeting area offers students a relaxed and "homey" feel.

In this meeting area, the teacher has full access to an LCD screen allowing her to easily display writing as she teaches her lesson.

Writer's notebooks are an important tool for writers in grades 3–8. Writer's notebooks are used daily during writing workshop, but are also often used during the active engagement portion of the minilesson. In addition to entries, charts and other tools can be kept in a writer's notebook, or can be kept in a two-pocket folder.

Anchor charts allow teachers to jot down key teaching points from minilessons throughout a unit of study. These charts are kept on display so children can refer back to them as they work.

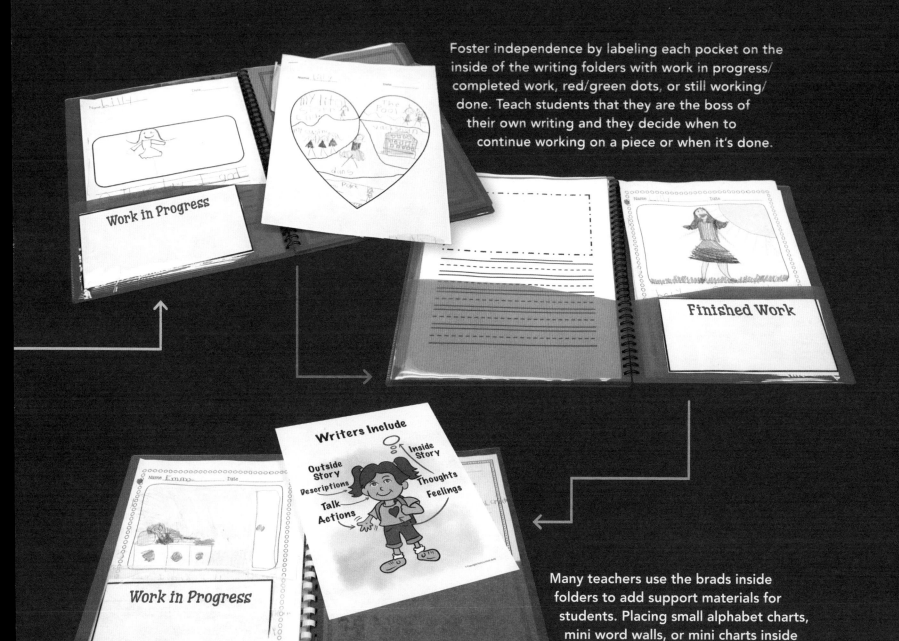

Foster independence by labeling each pocket on the inside of the writing folders with work in progress/completed work, red/green dots, or still working/done. Teach students that they are the boss of their own writing and they decide when to continue working on a piece or when it's done.

Work in Progress

Finished Work

Writers Include

Outside Story Descriptions

Inside Story

Thoughts Feelings

Talk Actions

Work in Progress

Many teachers use the brads inside folders to add support materials for students. Placing small alphabet charts, mini word walls, or mini charts inside a plastic sleeve places important information at a student's fingertips.

Writers in K–2 need a wide variety of paper choices. We believe in using a gradient of paper throughout the year. Introducing paper with fewer lines early, and adding choices with more and more writing lines later, encourages students to write more. Simply put: the paper is the plan.

We don't want to be the paper passer outers during workshop. To allow us to step back from this tedious role, we provide students with access to all they need to write in our classroom writing center. The materials in these centers vary with the age of our students but common materials include paper, pens, staplers, tape, sticky notes, colored pencils, markers, tape, strips of paper to add on writing, and access to our favorite mentor texts.

Why Are Minilessons Mini?

In a whole-group minilesson, your goal is to teach students one thing in a very short amount of time—about ten minutes. Why? Recent research on attention span shows students are more distracted and less able to pay attention when lessons go beyond ten minutes. In a Hechinger report citing a 2016 peer-reviewed study in the journal *Learning and Instruction*, the authors stated: "Length of lesson matters, too. Students went off task more often as an instructional activity increased beyond 10 minutes. Indeed, the researchers found that 25 percent of instructional activities lasted longer than 17 minutes. That's longer than the typical adult attention span of 15 minutes, according to Karrie Godwin, a professor at Kent State University, and one of the lead authors of the study" (Hechinger Report 2017).

Eric Jensen's *Teaching with the Brain in Mind* (2005) informs and influences the ideas we bring to teaching minilessons. Jensen talks about bringing brevity to our lessons because the human brain is poor at nonstop attention. He provides us with the following guidelines for direct instruction:

> " Cut the length of focused attention time expected or required. Remember that the human brain is poor at nonstop attention. It needs time for processing and rest after learning.
>
> **Eric Jensen (2005)**

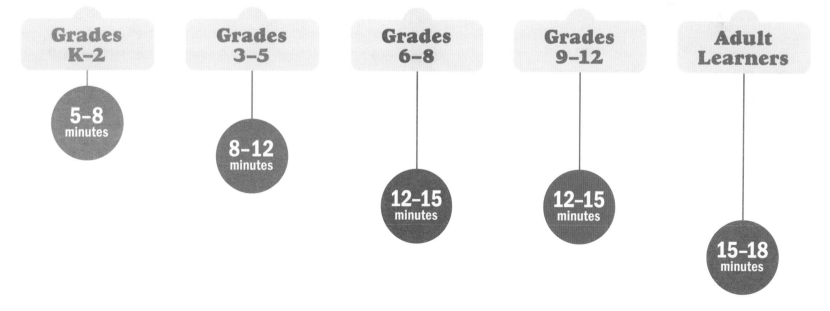

Grades K–2	Grades 3–5	Grades 6–8	Grades 9–12	Adult Learners
5–8 minutes	8–12 minutes	12–15 minutes	12–15 minutes	15–18 minutes

We want to consider the need for relevance within a lesson and time for processing after a lesson. When we stick to a ten-minute minilesson, we leave time for students to process that lesson during independent writing time. This is true for any teacher, in any grade level. Think of Kristin and Tracy, each in their own classrooms, each with a different group of students with different strengths and needs, each delivering a minilesson that was taught in response to their students' needs, but always in about a ten-minute time frame.

> **"**
>
> A school's emotional environment is even more vital. Whether schools are open or forbidding, friendly or unwelcoming, joyful or fearful, largely depends on the policies and practices enacted in a school as a whole and in particular classrooms.
>
> **Sonia Nieto (2013)**

Tip

Before your next professional development or grade-level meeting, ask teachers to record themselves teaching a minilesson and examine the recording for timing. As they listen or view the recording, they should consider the following questions:

1. How long was your minilesson? Were you able to keep it to about ten minutes?

2. If not, which parts went too long?

3. Why were certain parts too long?

   a. Did you ask questions during the connection?

   b. Was the teaching point unclear, causing you to over-teach? Or, did you teach with multiple examples?

   c. Did you ask too many students to share at the end of active engagement?

4. What can you do differently tomorrow?

When you meet, ask teachers to do a turn-and-talk or quick-write reflecting on what they noticed and what changes they plan to make to trim the length of their lessons. Ask volunteers to share their plans.

To Make Time for Independent Work

Minilessons are one part of a writing workshop. In a writing workshop, the ratio of time is such that student independent practice happens for the *majority* of the time. The minilesson lasts 10–15 minutes, and students spend the majority of the workshop writing or practicing what they learned. "We teach short so students can practice long" is an adage we live by. No matter how much time you have for writing, we recommend that the amount of time to write is at least double the amount of time you take to teach. Here are some guidelines when it comes to your writing workshop:

If the Time You Have to Teach Writing Is . . .	Your Minilesson and Share Time Is . . .		The Amount of Time Students Have to Write Is . . .
	Minilesson	Share	
35 minutes →	7–10 minutes	3 minutes	22–25 minutes
43 minutes →	10 minutes	3 minutes	30 minutes
50 minutes →	12–15 minutes	5 minutes	33 minutes

> **"**
>
> There is a lot to do in a minilesson. Still, most minilessons should take between five and ten minutes, with the occasional minilesson reaching fifteen minutes if it includes a discussion or if the students do a writing exercise. If, however, our minilessons take more time than this—and, consequently, take time away from students' independent writing—we defeat the purpose of the lessons. No matter how successful our minilessons may be in giving students information or persuading them to make what we've taught part of their writing agendas, they simply won't have the time they need to write and, through writing, learn how to do the work we've taught them.
>
> **Carl Anderson (2000)**

> # We teach short so students can practice long.

Tip

How do I keep my minilessons from becoming maxi-lessons?

The struggle is real: teaching a short, focused minilesson in only ten minutes is tough! We know, we've struggled with this ourselves. Here are a few tips we've found helpful as we work to make our teaching as concise as possible so our students have ample time to practice.

- Do *not* ask any questions you know the answer to—aka, "read my mind" questions.

- If lots of students are raising their hands to share, do a quick turn-and-talk.

- Make a plan!

- Stick to the structure and timing (connection: 1 minute, teaching: 3–5 minutes, active engagement: 2–3 minutes, link: 1 minute).

- If applicable, ask students to bring their writing folders and/or writing notebooks to the minilesson meeting area to create a smooth and efficient transition to active engagement.

- Use a timer!

To Make Sure Learning Occurs in Manageable Chunks

When we think about our writing curriculum for the year, it can feel overwhelming. There are many types of writing we need to teach, many concepts to cover. One way to make writing feel manageable is to break down concepts into smaller chunks. Let's take an argument writing unit. In upper elementary and middle school grades, writers of argumentation need to compose a text that contains:

1 a topic that is arguable

2 a thesis or stance on that argument

3 reasons why the writer takes that stance

4 evidence and factual information that support the reasons

5 some thinking that addresses the counterargument

6 ideas written in a cohesive and fluid way

That is one tall order!

> " In minilessons, we teach into our students' intentions. Our students are first deeply engaged in their self-sponsored work, and then we bring them together to learn what they need to know in order to do that work. This way, they stand a chance of being active meaning-makers, even during this bit of formal instruction.
>
> **Lucy Calkins (1994)**

It would be unreasonable to think that writers could digest and manage all of those expectations at once. Instead, we can create a series of lessons over time so that writers can learn the concepts and have plenty of time to practice what they learn. The way we manage that is to teach in smaller chunks. Each element of argument writing can be addressed in *separate* minilessons so only *one* concept is taught and practiced. That one concept might take one day or several days to teach. It depends on the needs of your students. The learning could go like this:

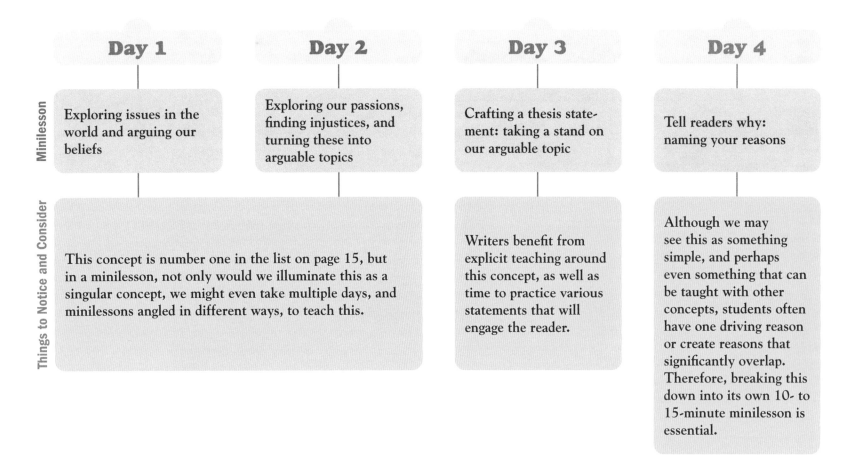

	Day 1	Day 2	Day 3	Day 4
Minilesson	Exploring issues in the world and arguing our beliefs	Exploring our passions, finding injustices, and turning these into arguable topics	Crafting a thesis statement: taking a stand on our arguable topic	Tell readers why: naming your reasons
Things to Notice and Consider	This concept is number one in the list on page 15, but in a minilesson, not only would we illuminate this as a singular concept, we might even take multiple days, and minilessons angled in different ways, to teach this.		Writers benefit from explicit teaching around this concept, as well as time to practice various statements that will engage the reader.	Although we may see this as something simple, and perhaps even something that can be taught with other concepts, students often have one driving reason or create reasons that significantly overlap. Therefore, breaking this down into its own 10- to 15-minute minilesson is essential.

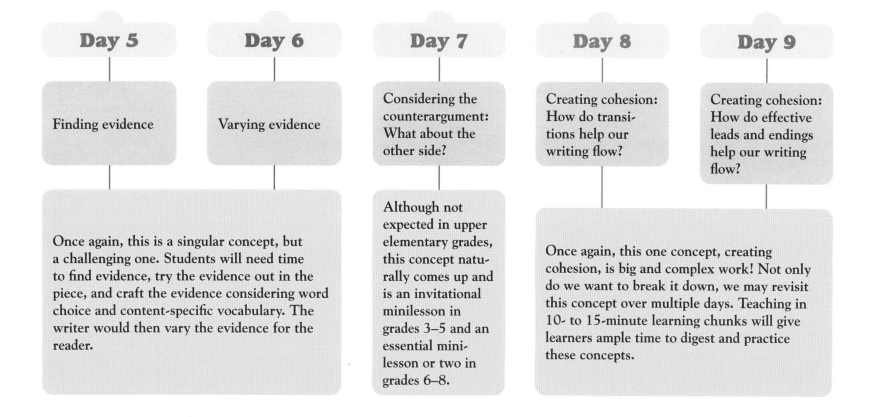

Day 5

Finding evidence

Once again, this is a singular concept, but a challenging one. Students will need time to find evidence, try the evidence out in the piece, and craft the evidence considering word choice and content-specific vocabulary. The writer would then vary the evidence for the reader.

Day 6

Varying evidence

Day 7

Considering the counterargument: What about the other side?

Although not expected in upper elementary grades, this concept naturally comes up and is an invitational minilesson in grades 3–5 and an essential mini-lesson or two in grades 6–8.

Day 8

Creating cohesion: How do transitions help our writing flow?

Once again, this one concept, creating cohesion, is big and complex work! Not only do we want to break it down, we may revisit this concept over multiple days. Teaching in 10- to 15-minute learning chunks will give learners ample time to digest and practice these concepts.

Day 9

Creating cohesion: How do effective leads and endings help our writing flow?

To Acknowledge That There Are Multiple Opportunities to Teach During the Writing Workshop

Minilessons are also mini so that we can create multiple teaching opportunities in a writing workshop: to a whole group during the minilesson, with individuals or small groups during the independent writing time, and again at the end of workshop during the share. Minilessons are a thread we weave into each part.

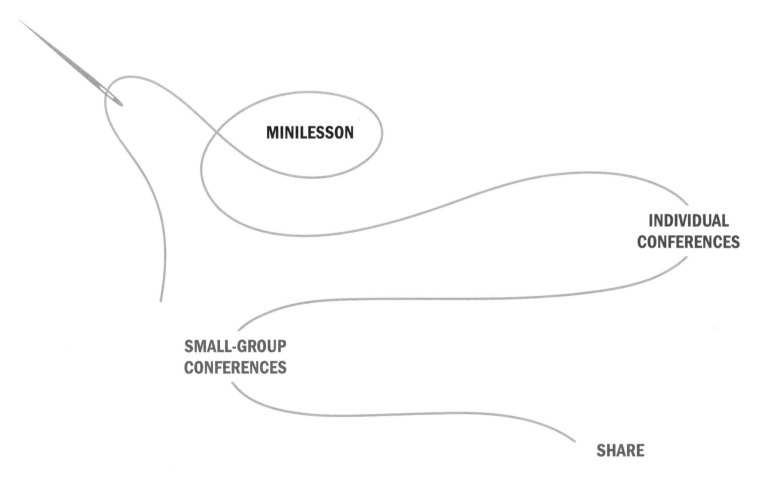

MINILESSON

INDIVIDUAL CONFERENCES

SMALL-GROUP CONFERENCES

SHARE

After the whole-group minilesson, we send students off to work. Students write independently as we confer with individuals and small groups. During one-to-one conferences we address the writing needs of an individual student. In small group conferences we can target instruction based on the needs of a group of students. In individual and small-group conferences, we can:

> draw on the work we have
> done in minilessons

> reteach a concept taught in
> previous minilessons

> teach students something new that may
> be taught in future minilessons

Whether you are working with a small group or an individual, the structure of the conference is similar to that of a minilesson. We call these parallel structures (Vitale-Reilly 2015).

Finally, the closing segment of the workshop, the share (we like to think of it as a wrap-up because it's an opportunity to teach and reflect) can circle back to what you taught in the whole-group minilesson, when the teaching point is reexamined and the teacher asks students to share with partners or the whole class how they applied the new strategy or technique.

Minilessons are a thread we weave into each part of workshop.

Inclusive Practices to Support Every Writer

Consistency matters with all students, but when we consider the learners in our classrooms with their diverse array of needs, consistency becomes even more important. Therefore, one way to address the needs of many of our students is to capitalize on consistency.

DRAWING ON THE WORK IN MINILESSONS

What Type of Learner Might Benefit from This Move?

- Students with language processing challenges, with or without individualized education plans (IEPs)
- Entering, emerging, or expanding English learners (ELs)

The Specific Move I Can Make

During a small-group session or conference, utilize a:
- tool
- text
- specific phrase from a previous minilesson

Why?

- Consistent language scaffolds and smooths students' ability to process since the language is known and familiar.
- Students can use the schema built in the minilesson during the differentiated instruction.

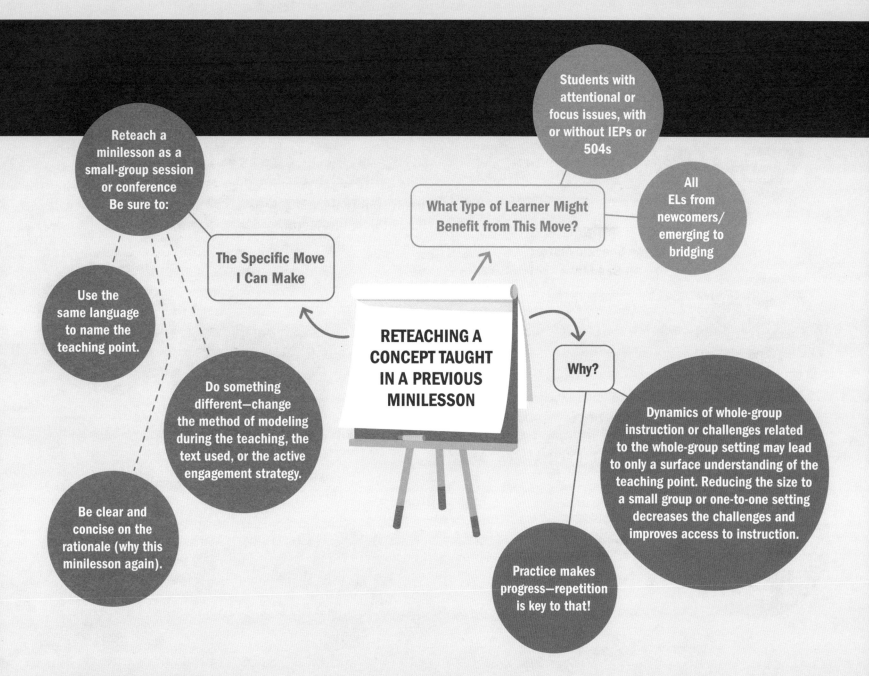

Reteach a minilesson as a small-group session or conference
Be sure to:

Use the same language to name the teaching point.

Do something different—change the method of modeling during the teaching, the text used, or the active engagement strategy.

Be clear and concise on the rationale (why this minilesson again).

The Specific Move I Can Make

What Type of Learner Might Benefit from This Move?

Students with attentional or focus issues, with or without IEPs or 504s

All ELs from newcomers/ emerging to bridging

RETEACHING A CONCEPT TAUGHT IN A PREVIOUS MINILESSON

Why?

Dynamics of whole-group instruction or challenges related to the whole-group setting may lead to only a surface understanding of the teaching point. Reducing the size to a small group or one-to-one setting decreases the challenges and improves access to instruction.

Practice makes progress—repetition is key to that!

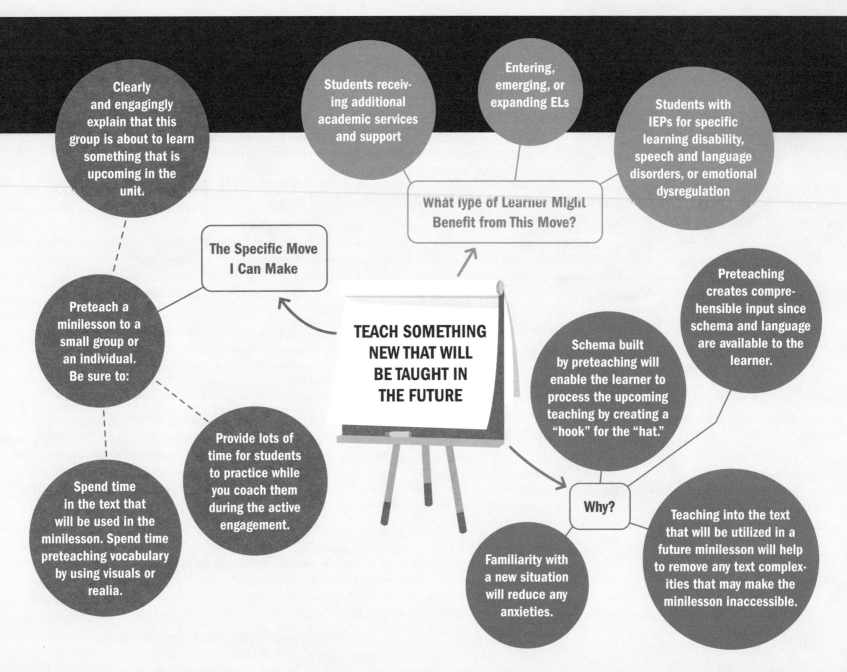

Clearly and engagingly explain that this group is about to learn something that is upcoming in the unit.

Students receiving additional academic services and support

Entering, emerging, or expanding ELs

Students with IEPs for specific learning disability, speech and language disorders, or emotional dysregulation

What Type of Learner Might Benefit from This Move?

The Specific Move I Can Make

Preteach a minilesson to a small group or an individual. Be sure to:

Spend time in the text that will be used in the minilesson. Spend time preteaching vocabulary by using visuals or realia.

Provide lots of time for students to practice while you coach them during the active engagement.

TEACH SOMETHING NEW THAT WILL BE TAUGHT IN THE FUTURE

Schema built by preteaching will enable the learner to process the upcoming teaching by creating a "hook" for the "hat."

Preteaching creates comprehensible input since schema and language are available to the learner.

Why?

Familiarity with a new situation will reduce any anxieties.

Teaching into the text that will be utilized in a future minilesson will help to remove any text complexities that may make the minilesson inaccessible.

A minilesson framework allows teachers to connect a lesson—often one that is mandated by a set of standards, a district curriculum, or a grade-level unit plan— to the cultural knowledge and experiences of the students.

Chapter 2

Building a Minilesson Toolbox and Deciding What to Teach

IT'S A FEW MINUTES AFTER dismissal on a Friday afternoon. Sandy sits at a table in her classroom with her plan book and a pile of student writing. She reviews her plans for the next week and then examines her students' writing to see if the lessons she planned at the start of the unit still seem appropriate. She reads her students' writing and begins sorting them into piles. Patterns emerge quickly. She labels some sticky notes to mark each pile. She notices her students are doing well stating their opinions and organizing their reviews into sections, but the reviews are not convincing because students are not supporting their opinions with enough details. The pile labeled "elaboration" grows steadily larger. Soon her teaching decision becomes obvious—more lessons on elaboration are in order. She already has two elaboration lessons planned but realizes she needs more. But what strategies will help this group the most?

She grabs her own writing notebook, the mentor texts she's given her students, and her favorite professional book. She wonders, "What did I do to elaborate when I wrote my book review?" After noticing the moves she made in her own writing, Sandy turns to the pile of mentor texts. "What were some of the craft moves our mentor authors used?" As another go-to, Sandy always turns to the experts that fuel her thinking and asks, "What elaboration strategies are mentioned in my favorite professional books?" After studying these three types of texts, she identifies several key elaboration strategies. She jots the new teaching points into her plan book—crossing out previous lessons she'd mapped out with her teaching team. She smiles, confident the changes she made to her minilessons are based on what she has learned about writing.

To identify specific teaching strategies, Sandy needed to learn things about writing to add to her minilesson toolbox. You can learn things about writing by:

doing your own writing and reflecting	studying mentor texts	studying what authors have to say about writing	studying professional texts

> **"**
>
> Write yourself. Invite children to do something you're already doing. If you're not doing it, "Hey," the kids say, "I can't wait to grow up and not have to write, like you." They know. And for the short term and the long term, you'll be doing yourself a favor by writing. All of us need it as a survival tool in a very complex world. The wonderful thing about writing is that it separates the meaningless and the trivial from what is really important. So we need it for ourselves and then we need to invite children to do what we're doing. You can't ask someone to sing a duet with you until you know the tune yourself.
>
> **Don Graves (n.d.)**

You must go through the same process you're asking students to go through. If your students are writing reviews, you should be writing reviews too.

Do Your Own Writing and Reflecting

When Lisa's son was little, she took him to a swim coach to learn to swim. The coach got into the pool with Jack and taught him to float and paddle. Lisa observed each lesson and noted how the coach demonstrated the moves Jack should make. She also noticed that as the coach demonstrated, she articulated her process for him by naming what she did and describing how she did it. The coach was able to both show and tell Jack how to swim because she swam herself. Lisa would never have taken her son to a coach who never got in the pool. So it is with writing: if you want to teach kids to write, you need to get in the pool! You must go through the same process you're asking students to go through. If your students are writing reviews, you should be writing reviews too. And, as you write, be reflective—notice what you did and how you did it. Pay attention to the process and habits that made writing work for you. For example, when drafting a piece, ask yourself, "What did I do? How did I get started? What strategies did I use to get an idea? What helped me stay focused and keep writing? What did I do when things got difficult?" Reflecting on your process allows you to extrapolate key teaching points and turn them into actionable steps you can share in your minilessons.

The best teachers we know are always in the pool—whatever they ask students to do, they dive in and test the water first.

Topic: Writing Book Reviews

Question

How did I get started?

My Answer

I made a T-chart listing important characters and moments from the book and what I thought about each character and moment.

How That Helps Me Know What to Teach in a Minilesson

There are different ways to start writing. I can share my way of getting started, but I want to make sure students have other options. Maybe they can share methods that work for them.

When/Where in the Writing Process Will I Teach This Minilesson?

Rehearsal/gathering ideas or drafting

Question	**My Answer**	**Question**	**My Answer**
What strategies did I use to get an idea?	I looked at the class list of read-alouds and my reading response book and made a list of books I knew. I then went back and starred the books I loved and felt strongly about. Then I circled a couple of my favorites and jotted reasons why I like them off to the side. In the end, I chose the book that I had the strongest reaction to.	What helped me stay focused and keep writing?	I worked to keep my pencil moving across the page. I kept in mind that the first draft doesn't need to be perfect—there will be time to make it better later.

How That Helps Me Know What to Teach in a Minilesson

Making lists often helps me make decisions about what to write and why. Lists can also help students decide what they want to write about and make sure it is something they feel strongly about.

When/Where in the Writing Process Will I Teach This Minilesson?

Rehearsal/gathering ideas/ brainstorming

How That Helps Me Know What to Teach in a Minilesson

Writers need to realize that their first drafts will be messy and unfinished. It's important to know that writing can be revised to make it better. The goal of drafting is to get something on the page to work with later.

When/Where in the Writing Process Will I Teach This Minilesson?

Drafting

continues

Question

What did I do when things got difficult?

How That Helps Me Know What to Teach in a Minilesson

Reading like a writer is an effective way to help you get unstuck and add different techniques into your piece.

My Answer

When I get stuck, it helps me to read a mentor text. I re-read a favorite review with sticky notes in hand. As I read, I look at the ways the reviewer structures their text and the craft moves they use. I make notes of things I might want to try in my draft.

When/Where in the Writing Process Will I Teach This Minilesson?

Revision

Online Resource 2.1
Write and Reflect Chart

Write and Reflect Chart

Topic:

Question	My Answer	How That Helps Me Know What to Teach in a Minilesson	When/Where in the Writing Process Will I Teach This Minilesson?

Support for teacher writers is only a click away. A few of our favorite places to encourage and support teachers as they write include:

> Kate Messner's #TeachersWrite

> Linda Urban's #WriteDaily30Challenge

> #TeachWrite Chat

> Two Writing Teachers Slice of Life Challenge

Work with your peers and organize a teacher's writing club. Set a time to meet each month to discuss your writing and learn about being a writer. A good way to get teachers writing is to try an activity by literacy coach Jennifer Allen. In *Becoming a Literacy Leader* (2006), Allen suggests launching teachers into the writing process with "My Life in Seven Stories." In this idea-generating strategy, teachers begin by considering the seven key stories of their life. At each subsequent meeting, the literacy leader or coach models strategies to navigate the writing process or improve writing. As with any writing workshop, teachers are invited to share their ongoing work with their peers and receive feedback. The goal is to get teachers doing what we ask students to do each day so they can bring that understanding into their work with kids.

Study Mentor Texts to Learn About Genre and Craft

In addition to learning to teach writing by writing, you can learn a lot about teaching writing by reading. Before embarking on a unit of study, gather a few examples of the kind of writing you want your kids to do and read through them. Studying the work of published authors, or using them as mentors, is one of the best ways to understand what it means to write well. Before you study mentor texts with your students, you'll want to study them on your own or with a colleague. It helps to use a predictable process. One helpful protocol is to Notice, Name, and Note (Eickholdt 2015; Ray 1999).

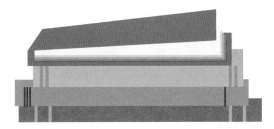

1
NOTICE

As you read, pay attention to the parts of the texts that stand out to you. Notice excerpts that cause an emotional response or paint a picture in your mind. The parts that make you laugh, cry, or sigh with delight—this is the craft of writing. Mark those parts with a sticky note or underline the words or passages.

2
NAME

What will you call that craft move? If you know the literary term for what you noticed, use that term (e.g., *alliteration, simile, personification*). It's OK if you don't know the literary term for a craft move. It is more important that you give it a name so that the craft move is repeatable. As you consider what to call a craft move, you will also want to think about all the other texts where you've seen this technique used so you can share them with your students.

3
NOTE

As a final step, you will want to consider why the craft move was chosen by the writer. Writers purposefully choose to use certain techniques. Understanding why the writer chose a craft move, or why it's notable, helps you decide if and when you will teach it to your students. It also helps you explain to them why they might want to use this strategy in their own writing.

Here's what it might look like:

NOTICE

Last Stop on Market Street
by Matt de la Peña

CJ: "How come we always gotta go here after church? Miquel and Colby never have to go nowhere."

Nana: "I feel sorry for those boys. They'll never get to meet Mr. Bobo or the Sunglasses man."

CJ: "How come it's always so dirty over here?"

Nana: "Sometimes when you are surrounded by dirt, CJ, you're a better witness for what's beautiful."

NAME

Showing, not telling, using dialogue

NOTE

Reveals the main character's feelings and the relationship between the two characters

WHEN/WHERE IN THE WRITING PROCESS WILL I TEACH THIS MINILESSON?

When I need to teach students to revise a narrative piece of writing—one way to elaborate is to use dialogue.

NOTICE

Jabari Jumps
by Gaia Cornwell

He walked all the way to the end of the board. His toes curled around the rough edge. Jabari looked out, as far as he could see. He felt like he was ready. "I love surprises," he whispered.

He took a deep breath and spread his arms and bent his knees.

Then he sprang up!

Up off the board!

Flying!

NAME

Describing precise character actions. What are your hands, feet, and face doing? (Anderson 2009)

NOTE

Helps the reader envision the character

WHEN/WHERE IN THE WRITING PROCESS WILL I TEACH THIS MINILESSON?

As students draft, I can teach them to use this technique to write with detail.

Studying the work of published authors is one of the best ways to understand what it means to write well.

Online Resource 2.2
Notice, Name, Note Chart

Notice, Name, Note Chart			
Notice	Name	Note	When/Where in the Writing Process Will I Teach This Minilesson?

> **With a room full of authors to help us, teaching writing doesn't have to be so lonely.**
>
> **Katie Wood Ray (1999)**

Inclusive Practices to Support Every Writer

When studying mentor texts for potential teaching ideas, be sure to consider any challenges you think your learners may have. Consider the following as you move through the Notice, Name, and Note protocol:

1

Notice the text as per the recommended process previously described. To support this work, consider ways to make the text more accessible: provide students with a copy of the text, alter the text to make it more accessible (e.g., add more space to the page or number the sections), or project the text in a prominent way and position learners close to the projected text so that the visual is clear and the page accessible. In addition, consider the use of texts in a student's first language. Allow them to read/listen to the text in their native language as they "notice" the parts that stand out. The name and note will occur in English, however this translanguaging will build upon the first language in powerful ways!

2

Name the craft move. As suggested previously, consider the literary term, but also consider naming the term in a way that is most accessible to your students and their needs. For example, some teachers consider student-friendly terms such as calling alliteration "same sounding starts." The term same sounding starts provides context and immediate understanding since the name defines the technique. Others choose to use both the literary term and the student-friendly term. This way, students understand the context for when the use of the literary term is expected to be used. In addition, consider a student's native language, cognates or terms that might be culturally relevant (whether connecting to language and culture or by using pop culture).

3

Note. As you consider the why behind each craft move, think about your students and their zone of proximal development. Be sure to state the why in a way that is both developmentally appropriate and within reach linguistically and conceptually. In addition, consider any learning challenges students may have as well as the English language acquisition level of your students. As you consider teaching this craft move, begin to imagine any scaffolds you might put into place to make this successful. Possible scaffolds include using concrete and sparse language and using an If . . . Then . . . structure written in the second person. E.g., If your lead doesn't paint a picture in your mind, then you might want to include a description of the setting.

Study What Authors Have to Say About Writing

You can read what published authors have to say about writing to gain insight into their process and habits. You can also look for examples of how authors revise their writing. Many authors have written books providing insight into their writing work. Reading what other writers have to say about writing can provide valuable information and allows you to see new ways to navigate the writing process.

> "
> Writing is primarily not a matter of talent, of dedication, of vision, of vocabulary, of style, but simply a matter of sitting. The writer is a person who writes.
>
> Donald Murray (2009)

Some of Our Favorite Books on Writing by Writers

Writing Down the Bones: Freeing the Writer Within by Natalie Goldberg

On Writing: A Memoir of the Craft by Stephen King

On Writing Well: An Informal Guide to Writing Nonfiction by William Zinsser

Bird by Bird: Some Instructions on Writing and Life by Anne Lamott

This Year You Write Your Novel by Walter Mosley

Steering the Craft by Ursula Le Guin

Some Online Resources to Learn More About the Writing Process and Revision

https://www.thoughtco.com/writers-on-rewriting-1689262

https://www.theatlantic.com/entertainment/archive/2011/06/first-drafts-gary-sotos-talking-to-myself-and-sunday-without-clouds/241077

https://www.nieonline.com/thelearningforum/2012writers.cfm

http://www.ushistory.org/declaration/document/rough.html

Many authors on Twitter offer more frequent reflections about their ongoing writing work. Reading what they have to say about the writing process can be very informative.

Some Authors to Follow

Amy VanDerwater
(@amylvpoemfarm)

Stephen King
(@StephenKing)

J.K. Rowling
(@jk_rowling)

Jason Reynolds
(@JasonReynolds83)

Jacqueline Woodson
(@JackieWoodson)

Aisha Saeed
(@aishacs)

Kwame Alexander
(@kwamealexander)

Gene Luen Yang
(@geneluenyang)

Marie Lu
(@Marie_Lu)

Minh Le
(@bottomshelfbks)

Renée Watson
(@reneewauthor)

> **"**
>
> Writers are just like everyone else—except for one big difference. Most people go through life experiencing daily thoughts and feelings, noticing and observing the world around them. But writers record these thoughts and observations.
>
> **Ralph Fletcher (2003)**

When we study what authors have to say about writing, it might change what we teach in a minilesson.

KWAME ALEXANDER TWEET

RENÉE WATSON AND JASON REYNOLDS:
Video Interview at the Langston Hughes House

J.K. ROWLING QUOTE

What Authors Have Said

A kid asked me "What are some of your techniques for brainstorming?"

I answered: Butt. In. Chair. Also, I like to throw ideas around with my writing . . .

"When I'm writing prose I read a lot of poetry. And when I'm writing poetry I read a lot of narrative work and prose."

—Renée Watson

"I can write anywhere. I made up the names of the characters on a sick bag while I was on an airplane. I told this to a group of kids and a boy said, 'Ah, no, that's disgusting.' And I said, 'Well, I hadn't used the sick bag.'"

How It Impacts *What I Teach*

Writers don't wait for inspiration— they write each day. Teach students to make time for writing each day (and provide time in class every day).

Writers read before they write. Not only do they read the kind of writing they are working on, they read other genres to improve their craft. Teach students to study all kinds of mentor texts for lessons.

Writers think about writing all the time. It is a good idea to always carry a pen and a small notebook with you to record ideas.

Study Professional Texts About Writing

We are all better when we stand on the shoulders of the giants who have blazed a trail before us. With this in mind, one of the ways to find ideas for minilessons is to study the work of educators you think are "teaching giants." We know it's a personal journey to identify the professional texts or authors you find most helpful. Just to get you started, here are a few of our favorite professional texts about writing:

Professional Texts About Writing

Nonfiction Craft Lessons, JoAnn Portalupi and Ralph Fletcher (2001)

Study Driven, Katie Wood Ray (2006)

The Big Book of Details: 46 Moves for Teaching Writers to Elaborate, Roz Linder (2016)

Awakening the Heart: Exploring Poetry in Elementary and Middle School, Georgia Heard (1999)

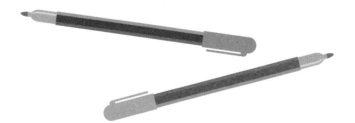

> **"**
> If you want to be a writer, you must do two things above all others: read a lot and write a lot. There's no way around these two things that I'm aware of, no shortcut.
>
> Stephen King (2000)

What Authors Have Said

JOANN PORTALUPI AND RALPH FLETCHER
Nonfiction Craft Lessons: Teaching Informational Writing K–8 (2001)

> Early in the process we want students to avoid writing the report and become an expert on the subject. Later, once they are walking resources on their topics, they can turn their attention toward writing about them. (9)

ROZ LINDER
The Big Book of Details: 46 Moves for Teaching Writers to Elaborate (2016)

> The Action Clues move describes a series of actions that offer the reader clues to interpret and make their own inferences about. (27)

GEORGIA HEARD
Awakening the Heart: Exploring Poetry in Elementary and Middle School (1999)

> Poetry is about recognizing and paying attention to our inner lives—our memories, hopes, doubts, questions, fears, joys—and the image is the hook we find to hang the poem on. (66)

How It Impacts *What I Teach*

Students need to explore before they write; make lists, capture words and phrases, collect facts.

Writers show how characters feel through specific actions. Teaching students to use actions to reveal a character's inner thoughts is a powerful way to show, not tell.

Poets often begin writing around a feeling, and an image is a good way to start.

How Do I Know *What* to Teach in a Minilesson?

We are often asked for a list of our favorite minilessons—lessons that seem essential to teach in a year of writing.

There are many factors that go into planning a year of minilessons, and the first step is to engage in some of the steps we've suggested. After that, we consider the following:

Required Curriculum

What kinds of writing are you required to teach in your district? Since the inception of the Common Core State Standards, and in the recent revisions that most states have implemented, the majority of states now require instruction in the three primary types of writing: argumentative/opinion, informational, and narrative. What genres will you teach your kids to help them meet the new standards? What writing curriculum does your school use? How will you implement that work?

Your Work with Your Grade-Level Team

What kinds of writing do you and your peers want and need to teach? Is your grade level known for teaching a certain unit? Do your kids come to you needing more instruction in one area or type of writing?

Your Students' Needs and Interests

What are your students' favorite genres? Do they love reading graphic novels? Perhaps a unit on comic book writing is in order. Do they need practice revising? Perhaps a unit on revision is necessary.

Your Interests as a Writing Teacher

Do you have favorite units of study? Are you itching to try something new you've read about? Do you excel at teaching one genre in particular?

For us, minilessons are always organized in units of study—a period of approximately 4–5 weeks—where each lesson is centered around a big idea. In writing, the big idea can be a genre, author, or even a habit or element of the writing process. Once we consider the unit frames to our year, we plan for essential minilessons. Here are what we consider to be essential minilessons that can be incorporated into any unit frame:

Habits of Writers

1. FIND IDEAS

General Lesson

Keep your notebook with you as you read to capture any and all interesting thoughts. Reading is fertile ground for ideas.

Genre-Specific Lesson: Fiction

Take your notebook with you out into the world and people watch. Create character sketches and backstories for the interesting people you see.

Genre-Specific Lesson: Opinion/Argument Writing

Keep your notebook with you as you watch the evening news. What are topics that pose controversy? In which of those topics would you like to see change?

2. KEEP A WRITER'S NOTEBOOK

General Lesson

Personalize your writing notebook with pictures, stickers, and other images that are special to you. These images will help you generate ideas for writing later.

Genre-Specific Lesson: Fiction

Collect beautiful lines from your favorite stories. Borrow a line and use it in your writing.

Genre-Specific Lesson: Opinion/Argument Writing

Jot down issues that you feel strongly about at home, at school, and in the world. Write an entry for each to explore your thinking.

3. STUDY OTHER AUTHORS

General Lesson

Study your favorite author's writing habits or office work. How do they find time to write each day? How do they use a notebook? What tools do they use? Try adopting some of their habits.

Genre-Specific Lesson: Fiction

Find a fiction piece you love. Keep this mentor text next to as you write to help you choose structures and craft moves to add to your piece.

Genre-Specific Lesson: Opinion/ Argument Writing

Find an opinion piece you love. Keep this mentor text next to you as you write to help you choose structures and craft moves to add to your piece.

4. FIND THE RIGHT TOOL

General Lesson

Experiment with the different writing utensils in the classroom. Do you prefer writing with a pencil, a flair pen, or fine-tipped marker? What makes your writing flow?

Genre-Specific Lesson: Fiction

Writers collect words around their topic. Create a personalized list of beautiful words you could include in your stories.

Genre-Specific Lesson: Opinion/ Argument Writing

Writers research topics before writing. How will you collect your research? Will you use sticky notes, index cards, or file folders? Find your research tools and methods.

continues

(continued)

5. WRITE EVERY DAY

General Lesson

Experiment with writing in different parts of the classroom. Find a spot where you feel comfortable and able to write for extended periods of time.

Genre-Specific Lesson: Fiction

Make a goal to write more each day. Put an X on your page and write down to it. Move the X down your paper, adding more to your story each day.

Genre-Specific Lesson: Opinion/Argument Writing

Make a plan for your writing each day. What section or parts will you complete? Jot some notes in the margin earmarking sections for the thesis, reasons, or evidence to remind yourself of your goal.

Process of Writing

1. REHEARSAL

General Lesson

What ideas resonate with you? Writers have territories they write about again and again (Atwell 1998). What are yours? Create territories and then ideas—moments or times—that go with that territory.

Genre-Specific Lesson: Informational Feature Article

Take an idea from your expert list and orally rehearse by teaching someone else about your idea. After teaching, start writing!

Genre-Specific Lesson: Poetry

Poets write from the heart about things they care about. Take an idea from your heart map—a person, place, or special hobby—(Heard 1999) and rehearse the idea by creating a list of what you love about that person, place, or special hobby.

2. DRAFTING

General Lesson

Don't worry about making your writing perfect out of the gate; instead focus on keeping your pencil moving. Get something down to work with later.

Genre-Specific Lesson: Informational Feature Article

Use sketching to move your writing along. Write a bit, sketch a bit, and write some more.

Genre-Specific Lesson: Poetry

Pause as you draft to reread. Rereading will help you refocus your writing and pausing at certain places will help you begin to imagine the line breaks in your poem.

continues

3. REVISION

General Lesson

Read your draft aloud, listen to how it sounds, and revise wherever the sound feels a bit off.

Genre-Specific Lesson:
Informational Feature Article

Make a "map" of the sections of your draft to help you consider whether they are in the most logical order.

Genre-Specific Lesson: Poetry

Once you have a draft, experiment with the line breaks to see if moving them changes the look or sound of the poem.

4. EDITING

General Lesson

Read your draft aloud and listen. Does it sound right or do you need to add directions for the reader in the form of punctuation?

Genre-Specific Lesson:
Informational Feature Article

Read your draft multiple times. Each time check that the punctuation in the features (e.g., parentheses around the words' pronunciation) is correct.

Genre-Specific Lesson: Poetry

Read your piece and circle all the words you know you didn't spell correctly. Find the correct spelling in books, on the word wall, or using other resources.

Craft of Writing

1. FOCUS

General Lesson

Ask yourself, "So what? So why am I writing about this topic?" (Atwell 1998). Write down your answer to this question and use it not only to guide your writing, but also help get to the heart of your writing—the focal point.

Genre-Specific Lesson: Argument Writing

Jot down a list of titles for your piece. Examine them closely and choose the one that best supports your argument. Keep this title in mind as you angle your piece.

Genre-Specific Lesson: Personal Narrative

Think about your story. Are you writing about something that occurred in a large time span (a day or more)? If so, narrow your focus by limiting the time to something that occurred in 20–30 minutes.

continues

2. STRUCTURE

General Lesson

One of the most important decisions a writer makes is how to organize their piece. Organization to a writer is like architecture to a builder—you need to decide the parts and how they will fit and flow together.

Genre-Specific Lesson: Argument Writing

Write down all the reasons that support your argument. Check to be sure they are parallel. Use them to guide the architecture of the piece.

Genre-Specific Lesson: Personal Narrative

Check your beginning and ending to make sure they connect to one another.

3. ELABORATION

General Lesson

Add details to each part of your piece by adding to the pictures and/or adding to the words.

Genre-Specific Lesson: Argument Writing

Beef up your argument with personal experience. Add an anecdote to support one or more of your reasons.

Genre-Specific Lesson: Personal Narrative

Enhance your writing by adding the kind of detail that readers love—sensory images. Consider a sense that would add context to your writing (sound and sight work well!) and jot images based on that sense. Add those to your piece.

4. WORD CHOICE

General Lesson

Look for places in your draft where you've used adjectives. Could you replace them with more specific nouns?

Genre-Specific Lesson: Personal Narrative

If you have particular expressions or ways of saying things in your home, you might use these words in your writing. This can include adding phrases or sentences from a native language.

Genre-Specific Lesson: Argument Writing

Think about the tone you want to convey in your writing. Do you want to sound measured and reasonable? Angry? Sarcastic? Shocked? Funny? Consider whether your word choices are *best* for conveying that tone.

> **"**
>
> I write for two hours a day, but it's what I do for the other twenty-two hours that allows me to do that writing.
>
> **Donald Murray (2003)**

Now let's look closely at *how* to teach each part of a minilesson . . .

Chapter 3

The Connection

Minilesson Planning Template

Unit of Study:

Lesson Focus:

Connection (1 minute) Engage students: connect to previous teaching, connect to learner(s), capture interest, and activate prior knowledge. **Announce the teaching point.**	*We have been . . . Another way to . . .* *Today I am going to teach you . . .*
Teaching (5 minutes) Teach one thing. Choose the way to teach. **Demonstrate and model as much as you can.**	*Watch me as I . . .* *Did you see how I . . . ?*
Active Engagement (2–3 minutes) Quickly engage students by asking them to turn and talk to a partner, envision how it might go, or **try something quickly.**	*Now it is your turn to try.*
Link (1 minute) Restate the teaching point in one or two sentences. **Connect the teaching point to ongoing student work and independent practice.**	*Today we learned how to . . .*

From *A Teacher's Guide to Writing Workshop Minilessons*. Portsmouth, NH: Heinemann. © 2022 by Lisa Eickholdt and Patricia Vitale-Reilly. May be photocopied for classroom use.

THE FIRST PART OF A minilesson is called the connection. We like to think of the connection as the warm-up or anticipatory set (Hunter 1982, Hunter and Hunter 2004) of the lesson. Coaches help athletes warm up before a practice or game, choir conductors ask singers to individually or collectively warm up with scales or vocal exercises, and even writers might have a coach or mentor who helps them warm up with a quick writing exercise or writing prompt.

In a minilesson, the connection serves several purposes—it prepares and engages students, provides a clear teaching point, and leads us into our teaching. There are three types of connections: recap, tell a story, and use a metaphor.

Recap

This is the simplest, most concrete and efficient way to begin a minilesson. Start by briefly reminding students what they have been learning, and then connect that learning to what you want to teach them in today's lesson.

Quickly remind students what they have been working on and be specific.

> *Writers, we have spent the last couple of weeks writing personal narratives. We've learned how to find moments that matter and stretch out the most important parts by including specific actions. (Teacher pauses.) We can also stretch out the important parts of our writing in another way—by including inside story. The inside story is what you're thinking and feeling. So today I am going to teach you how to include inside story into your personal narratives by adding it into my story about Rosco.*

Use language that engages students and gives them context for the lesson.

Use consistent language to announce the teaching point.

Remember that *you* are providing a quick and engaging recap. The connection can get off track if you . . .

. . . turn it into a fishing expedition

What have we been doing as writers? Teacher calls on one student. *Yes, but what else?* Teacher calls on another student. *Jess, hold that thought and share that story later. Who else?* And by now, some are distracted, some are sidetracked, more than a minute has gone by, and students are still not warmed up and ready for this lesson! We know, we have been there!

. . . reteach yesterday's lesson

Yesterday, we focused on how to make our drafts draw the reader in from the first sentence. The teacher displays an anchor chart from yesterday's lesson. *The first strategy we looked at is _____. Remember, here we want to _____. Then we explored how to _____.* And now, students and teacher alike are down the rabbit hole of yesterday's lesson and five minutes have passed.

The recap connection can be used at the beginning of any minilesson, but it's especially helpful when you need to make sure you have plenty of time for the other parts of the lesson, because it's lean and efficient. And even if you don't start your minilesson this way, it's helpful to think about how the lesson you are getting ready to teach connects to the lessons you've been teaching and the work students are doing.

Video 3.1 Recap Type of Connection

Tip

If you are new to minilesson instruction or working to streamline your time, we recommend keeping your connections simple and using only one connection type: the recap. We encourage you to use this straightforward connection because it allows you to turn your time and attention to creating meaningful teaching and active engagement segments. As you become more comfortable with the minilesson timing and structure, you can begin to add stories and metaphors into your connection repertoire.

"

We all have a basic need for story, for organizing our experiences into tales of important happenings. Stories, these ubiquitous discourse forms, are of great interest in language and literacy education, particularly in light of the increasing sociocultural diversity of students in our classrooms. Through stories, teachers learn of their children's cultures, of their diverse experiences, and of their connections to family and friends. Moreover, through sharing stories—both children's own stories and those of professional authors—teacher and children create the potential for new connections that link them together inside a new tale.

Anne Haas Dyson and Celia Genishi (1994)

Tell a Story

This type of connection has a narrative flow. When you start the minilesson by telling a story about you, one student, or your collective group, it engages your learners and connects them to our universal humanity and experience. It also gives them personal context for their learning.

Make it concise and tell stories about writers in the classroom—this is powerful because it lets students know you are deeply engaged with them and their work.

Writers, I was having a conference with Lexi yesterday, and we were talking about how she tends to write around her topic a lot before she lands on exactly what she wants to say. Some believe that all that time and writing can be a waste, a distraction from what her task is. However, Lexi and I agree with Ralph Fletcher, who says that "brainstorming invites you into a quiet room where you can think deeply about your subject before you start shaping your text" (2003, 22). And so we agree, but Lexi was stuck. She was in that "let me do what I always do because it works" moment. Ever find yourself there? (Teacher pauses to notice some head shaking and thumbs up.) So I taught Lexi a new brainstorming strategy—a way she can brainstorm before she has a topic, to find seed ideas, and a way she can prewrite, or rehearse, an idea before creating a draft. Today, I am going to teach you a brainstorming strategy that you can use in either of those places.

Provide a story that is relevant to the teaching point and to the learners.

Use consistent language to announce the teaching point.

Remember that you are telling a story that is related to your teaching point. The connection can get off track if you . . .

. . . share irrelevant details

Writers, I was having a conference with Lexi yesterday, and we were talking about how she tends to write around her topic a lot before she lands on exactly what she wants to say. She showed me a few places where she does that and in the middle of showing me that, she noticed a few other moves she makes when writing around her topic. Teacher then shares details of the conference that are not relevant to the teaching point. *She showed me how she uses dialoguing (conversations between people and characters) and list writing (putting down details of the event). . .* Teacher and students alike are now lost inside of this story.

Video 3.2
Tell a Story Type of Connection

Inclusive Practices to Support Every Writer

Stories are engaging and help students see themselves as they draw upon the universality of experience in all of us. In that vein, consider the stories that you tell and their relevance to all your students. Using a familiar context will activate or quickly build background knowledge. In addition, be sure to use a clear voice, one that is quick enough to move the story along, but slow enough to be understood by all. Add gestures to essential parts of the connection to kinesthetically illustrate your point. In addition, be sure to name the teaching point in clear, concise language—one to two sentences at most. State the teaching point consistently at the end of the connection, and consider adding a gesture, movement, realia, or other visual to signal that you are stating the teaching point.

Use a Metaphor

When you start the minilesson with a metaphor, you share an idea or anecdote that compares the work you're asking students to do with something else that initially seems unrelated. This comparison should become clear to the learners and make them think.

Share a personal anecdote that will be a metaphor for your teaching point.

Writers, I was taking a walk yesterday with my nephew, and it was taking a long time. He stopped so many times to ask questions about a flower he had never seen before, or notice how fast a chipmunk was running. He even stopped to say hello to every other person we passed while we were walking. And when I thought about what he was doing, how he is the kind of person who takes a long time to take a walk because he is noticing everything about his world, I realized that is not just how people enjoy a walk, it is how a writer gets ideas. Writers are just like Evan—they stop to ask questions, observe a new flower, and notice how chipmunks run. So, today I am going to teach you how to be a wide-awake writer, one who sees the world as a potential list of writing ideas.

State the connection between the anecdote and the teaching point.

Use consistent language to announce the teaching point.

It is important that the metaphor fits the context of what you're teaching and also fits the developmental understanding of your learners. Metaphors can be effective and pack a punch, but can get off track if you . . .

. . . make them too esoteric

Writers, I was thinking about the artist, Gauguin, and how he used different mediums to create his art—oils, wood, stone. He was able to think about what he wanted to create and match purpose to medium. Writers are a lot like Gauguin . . . Students are too busy trying to find a context for Gauguin and various art mediums to understand the point of this connection.

Video 3.3
Metaphor Type of Connection

. . . move beyond the experiences of your students

Writers, when I was traveling all over Europe by train, I noticed that some travelers were organized and others weren't. The organized travelers packed lightly but had everything they might need. They knew exactly where things were in their backpack while other travelers had to pull out everything to find their toothbrush. It made me think about how writers are the same way . . . Students may be interested in this comparison, but the context for understanding is beyond their collective experiences and therefore will not set the stage for this minilesson.

End by Announcing the Teaching Point

The connection ends with an announcement of the teaching point. Though this announcement is short and comes at the end, its importance cannot be overstated for both you and your kids. When planning minilessons, teachers often begin by considering the types of connection (recap, story, or metaphor) they will utilize. Instead, we suggest you begin planning your minilessons by writing out the teaching point first. Think of a minilesson as an informational essay and the teaching point as the thesis statement. Once your thesis statement or big idea is clear in your mind, you can make a plan that ensures every other part of your lesson will support it. You will model your teaching point somehow in the teaching portion, students will practice it in some way during active engagement, and you will rearticulate it in the link. Being able to name your teaching point in one or two short sentences enables you to teach with clarity, and one of the most important things our students need is clear teaching. We want students to infer many things, but not what we are teaching.

> Being able to name your teaching point in one or two short sentences enables you to teach with clarity, and one of the most important things our students need is clear teaching.

How Do I Know What Kind of Connection to Use?

There really is no right or wrong type of connection in a minilesson. You want to choose the kind of connection that matches what you know about your comfort level with teaching, your students, and your teaching point.

If . . .	Then . . .
You are less experienced with the minilesson structure and want to elevate your minilesson practice quickly	
Your teaching is robust and you want to save a bit more time in the 10-minute minilesson for modeling	Choose the recap type of connection. These are simple, efficient, and effective.
Your active engagement is robust, and you want students to have the opportunity to quickly write in front of you	

If . . .	**Then . . .**	**If . . .**	**Then . . .**
Your learners respond well to storytelling	Choose the tell-a-story type of connection. Stories engage students quickly and allow you to use your voice, affect, cadence, and body to deeply connect and invite students into the minilesson.	Your goal is to present the teaching point as a concept	Use a metaphor as your type of connection. Metaphors represent deeper thinking and quickly get to the purpose of the teaching point.
You have a bank of stories connected to writing, or if you are the kind of teacher who is on the lookout for stories within your own community		Your goal is to connect new information to students' prior knowledge and experiences	
You want to quickly build familiarity and trust and want to use culturally responsive methods to invite students to be open to learning		You want to add an element of surprise to quickly engage your students	

Chapter 4

The Teaching

AFTER THE CONNECTION, YOU WILL want to demonstrate your teaching point. In this portion of the minilesson, you will want to *show* students how to do what it is you are teaching them. The key is to teach by doing, not by talking (Vitale-Reilly 2015). There are some options for how you can teach writers, but regardless of the method, there should be a *demonstration* of some kind. By *demonstration*, we don't mean that the teacher is always modeling or showing students how to implement a new strategy; we mean that the teacher *and* students are actively involved in the learning. There are a few different ways to demonstrate during the teaching portion of the writing minilesson.

Model with Your Own Writing

So much incidental learning happens when you write in front of students—they get to see you pause, think, struggle, and rethink—and this modeling matters just as much, if not more, than the writing itself. This method allows you to demonstrate not just product but process and strategy.

You use your own writing to demonstrate exactly what you want students to do in their writing. The key here is in the showing, although you will want to do two things—show students what to do, and tell them what you are doing by providing an ongoing narration. When using the teacher model type of demonstration, you'll write in the minilesson (rather than composing before), because students learn not just from the content (what you composed) but how you composed the content (what you think aloud, the mistakes you make, your process, when you pause, and so on). It's important to keep this demonstration short; we would never compose a whole piece in front of students. Instead, we might compose a lead or elaborate a section of a previously written text in some way.

Remember the following as you teach during the minilesson:

1

VERBAL ANNOTATION

You not only show students what to do, but also tell them. You will need to verbalize what you're doing and name the steps in the process.

2

CONSISTENT LANGUAGE

As you name the steps and what you are teaching a few times through the lesson, use the same language. For example, if we are teaching students that one way to elaborate in a nonnarrative is to use partner facts, we will want to say the name of this strategy, "partner facts," several times throughout the lesson.

3

REITERATE THE STEPS

End the teaching portion of the lesson with a recap of the process. This can be something like, "Did you see how I (recap steps in process)?"

Inclusive Practices to Support Every Writer

The first step to ensuring you are being inclusive of all your learners is to choose your teaching method with *all* students in mind. All four types of demonstrations are powerful and effective, but shared writing and using a mentor text with pictures are especially effective with newcomers and emergent ELs, and a teacher model or student-mentor-text model of a familiar text is particularly effective for students with speech and language challenges. Why? Shared writing is an inclusive and active practice where newcomers and emergent ELs can utilize their native language or a peer for support. Familiar texts, whether they are a teacher model or a student model, will scaffold students with speech and language challenges because the previous experience and familiarity will reduce the cognitive load on the learner. In addition, a teacher model is a live, active demonstration where the learner can benefit from the actions and gestures, not just the language used.

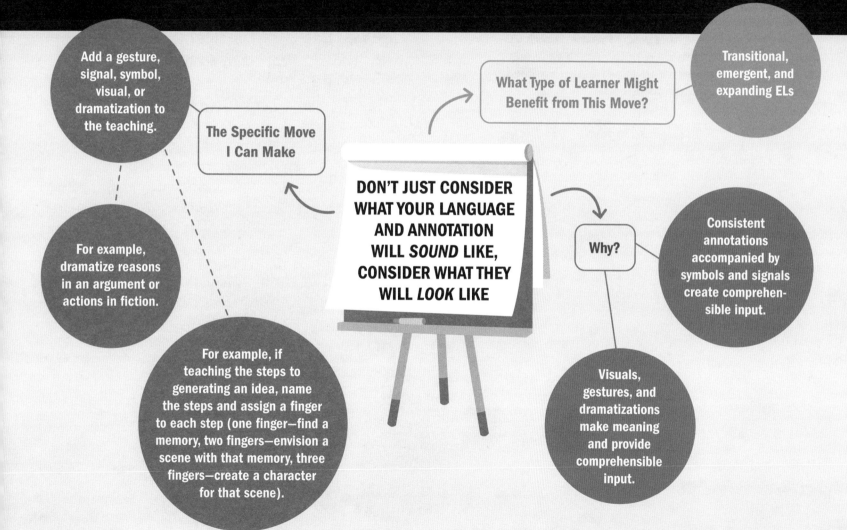

Add a gesture, signal, symbol, visual, or dramatization to the teaching.

The Specific Move I Can Make

For example, dramatize reasons in an argument or actions in fiction.

For example, if teaching the steps to generating an idea, name the steps and assign a finger to each step (one finger—find a memory, two fingers—envision a scene with that memory, three fingers—create a character for that scene).

DON'T JUST CONSIDER WHAT YOUR LANGUAGE AND ANNOTATION WILL *SOUND* LIKE, CONSIDER WHAT THEY WILL *LOOK* LIKE

What Type of Learner Might Benefit from This Move?

Transitional, emergent, and expanding ELs

Why?

Consistent annotations accompanied by symbols and signals create comprehensible input.

Visuals, gestures, and dramatizations make meaning and provide comprehensible input.

Let's say we want to teach our students how to use inside story in their narrative writing (Oxenhorn and Calkins 2003) using the teacher model method of demonstration. We would begin by showing students a piece of writing we had written on chart paper that is similar to what they've been writing, then we'd think aloud for them as we demonstrated adding inside story into our piece.

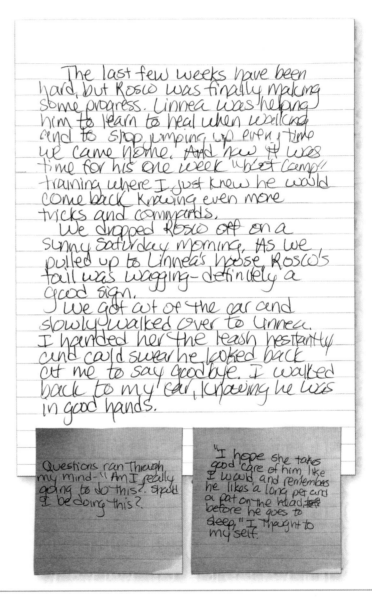

The last few weeks have been hard, but Rosco was finally making some progress. Linnea was helping him to learn to heal when walking and to stop jumping up every time we came home. And now it was time for his one week "boot camp" training where I just knew he would come back knowing even more tricks and commands.

We dropped Rosco off on a sunny Saturday morning. As we pulled up to Linnea's house, Rosco's tail was wagging—definitely a good sign.

We got out of the car and slowly walked over to Linnea. I handed her the leash hesitantly and could swear he looked back at me to say goodbye. I walked back to my car, knowing he was in good hands.

Questions ran through my mind—"Am I really going to do this? Should I be doing this?"

"I hope she takes good care of him like I would and remembers he likes a long pet and a pat on the head before he goes to sleep," I thought to myself.

What I Might Say

Writers, my story includes what happened when I took Rosco to the trainer for the first time, but it is missing the inside story: *my internal thinking and feelings.* (Teacher points to head and heart when she says "thinking" and "feeling.") *During the part where we get out of the car and I hand the leash over to Linnea, I am going to add* inside story: *my internal thinking.* "... slowly I walked over to Linnea. Questions ran through my mind: 'Am I really going to do this? Should I be doing this?' I handed her the leash hesitantly and could swear he looked back at me to say goodbye. 'I hope she takes care of him and remembers he likes a long pet and pat on the head before he goes to sleep,' I thought to myself." *Did you notice how I* (teacher lists the steps in the process using her fingers to demonstrate each step) *first found a part where I can add* inside story? *And then I decided whether I was adding internal thinking or what I was feeling. I then added it to my piece. You will want to do this in your piece when you find places where you can add* inside story.

> Consistent language

> Reiterate the steps

> Consistent language

Content This Method Best Serves

Writerly life components such as writing habits or process skills. Examples include:

WRITING HABITS

- Keep a writer's notebook
- Use the writing notebook as a tool instead of a collection container
- Generate writing ideas
- Live in the world as a "wide awake" writer
- Build writing stamina
- Vary topic choice
- Vary genre

PROCESS SKILLS

- Rehearse writing by using a tool such as a territories map (Atwell 1998); list; welcome to my world chart; or map of the heart (Heard 1999); or strategies such as oral rehearsal, writing in the margins to plan, or creating an idea box
- Draft writing by using a strategy such as planning the parts before writing, freewriting quickly down the page, cutting and pasting previous writing, or rereading and drafting
- Revise writing by adding, taking out, moving writing around, or using a craft technique

continues

(continued)

- Edit writing by using tools such as a checklist, word wall, or classroom editing center; or strategies such as rereading the text from the end to the beginning, or utilizing a writing partner

Tools You Need

- Your own writing idea; writing you plan to demonstrate in front of students
- Chart paper, paper with document camera, other projection device such as a SMART or Promethean Board

Video 4.1 Teacher Model

You not only show students what to do, but also tell them. You will need to verbalize what you're doing and name the steps in the process.

Use a Mentor Text

Nothing illuminates a thousand words better than a picture, or a mentor text!
Use a mentor text, or a powerfully written piece from another writer, as a tool to
demonstrate. The mentor text teaches you something you might want to know
and try in your own writing. There are three types of mentor texts we can use:

children's literature	**a piece of student writing**	**the teacher's writing (previously written)**

> **"**
>
> What they needed to see was not so much the after-image of what she had done
> the night before; the more valuable demonstration for them would have been the
> sloppy, insecure work at midnight at their teacher's kitchen table. I wondered
> whether it might have been better for Alicia to have gone on to bed and saved
> the actual writing work for class time, for the demonstration in front of students.
> They needed to see her look at her entry and say, "hmmm . . . how could this
> go? I could start with this part, but I have this other image in mind. Oh, well, I'll
> try it that way, and then do the other one next." They needed to see her work
> and reason through the muddle and worry that naturally comes at that point in
> writing; they could have used a demonstration from within the writing process
> rather than after the fact.
>
> **Randy Bomer (1998)**

Let's say you want to teach students to add details to their writing by describing what a character is doing in a narrative piece. You might use *Jabari Jumps* by Gaia Cornwall as a mentor text. We could choose a specific part and demonstrate how the author uses action, description, or dialogue to make the character come alive. Let me show you what I mean.

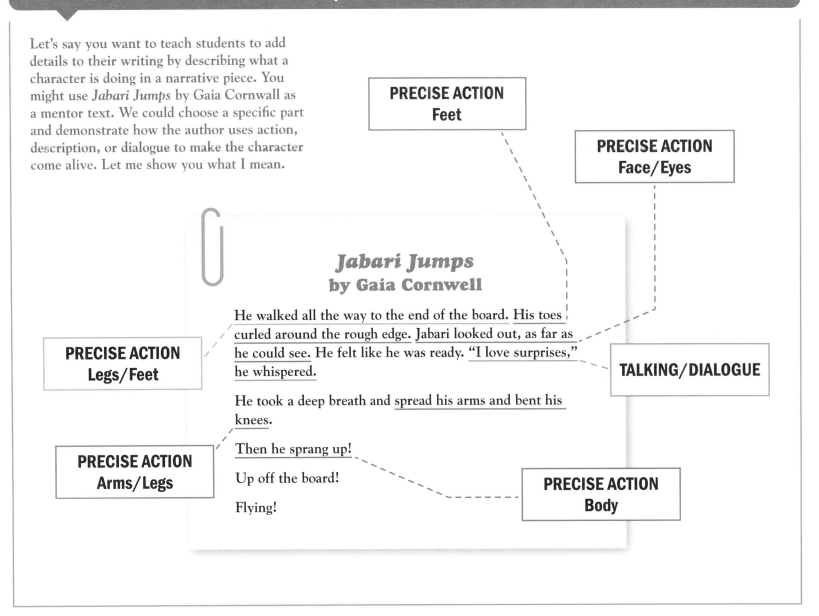

PRECISE ACTION
Feet

PRECISE ACTION
Face/Eyes

Jabari Jumps
by Gaia Cornwell

He walked all the way to the end of the board. His toes curled around the rough edge. Jabari looked out, as far as he could see. He felt like he was ready. "I love surprises," he whispered.

He took a deep breath and spread his arms and bent his knees.

Then he sprang up!

Up off the board!

Flying!

PRECISE ACTION
Legs/Feet

TALKING/DIALOGUE

PRECISE ACTION
Arms/Legs

PRECISE ACTION
Body

Writers, in the book Jabari Jumps, *Gaia Cornwall makes her character, Jabari, come to life by describing the character's precise body actions. She describes what his hands, feet, and face are doing during a key moment, the moment he decides to jump off the diving board. Let me show you what I mean. She writes, "He walked all the way to the end of the board. His toes curled around the rough edge. Jabari looked out, as far as he could see. He felt like he was ready, "I love surprises," he whispered. He took a deep breath and spread his arms and bent his knees. Then he sprang up! Up off the board! Flying!" Do you see how Gaia described this character's precise body actions? She told us what his hands, feet, and face were doing as he made the big jump. You will want to do this in your writing as it makes the text come alive in the reader's mind.*

Consistent language

Reiterate the steps

Consistent language

Craft Techniques: A mentor text is the perfect tool to demonstrate a craft technique based on one of the writing qualities. Craft techniques include:

FOCUS

- Zoom in on a moment and stretch it
- Pare down reasons to include only the most important
- Create chapters or sections so information is organized
- Add graphics or other features to zero in on the most important information such as adding headings, using highlights, or creating a zoom-box drawing

STRUCTURE

- Begin and end in the same way: circular structure
- Use language or features to signal transition
- Add a flashback or flashforward as a creative use of time

ELABORATION

- Add sensory images
- Add inside story
- Add dialogue or speech bubbles
- Add action

continues

(continued)

- Add different kinds of facts (action, telling, description)
- Add examples or quotes from an expert

WORD CHOICE

- Add descriptors (adjectives and adverbs)
- Use alliteration
- Vary verbs by replacing blah with vivid
- Use words from a native language
- Use discipline- or content-specific language

Tools You Need

- A mentor text (piece of children's literature, student writing, or your own previously written text)
- Chart paper, paper with document camera, other projection device such as a SMART or Promethean Board

Video 4.2 Mentor Text

Tip

Work through the process of notice, name, and note by studying a mentor text with other teachers. Place the text under a document camera or display it in some way to the group. As you read each page, go through the notice, name, and note protocol, annotating the text with sticky notes to mark each craft move. Write the name of the craft move on a sticky note and use it as a bookmark so you can easily refer back to it in lessons.

Piecing Me Together
by Renée Watson

Simile

I hear rattling, something like crumpling paper. I look to my left and see Lee Lee's hand is shaking. Her whole arm is having a fit. Her fist is clenching the bag like an anchor to keep her from falling to the ground. I tell her, "It's okay." I take her hand, but she pulls away. "It's okay, Lee Lee. Come on. Let's go."

Simile

Show, don't tell, characters' feelings

Show, don't tell, characters' feelings

Facilitate Shared Writing

Shared writing, an exercise in cocomposing texts alongside students, is an example of a shared practice. You create a piece of writing together with students. The teacher holds the pen, but all writers are minds-on and actively engaged in contributing to the text. This teaching method allows you to demonstrate not just product, but more importantly, process and strategy. So much incidental learning happens when you write *with* students; they participate in the learning and can grapple with the skill alongside you, the expert writer. Shared writing is especially engaging for reluctant writers, or learners who may become more passive during minilessons.

Example: Shared Writing

Let's say you want to teach writers that one way to begin a piece is to describe the setting. You'll begin by referring back to a shared piece of writing, something the class has worked on together. Then students brainstorm, in partnerships or as a whole class, different types of setting leads.

The Class Trip Gone Wrong

It was a seemingly typical Tuesday in 5T. Typical except for one exciting reason—we were finally going to be able to go on our class trip to Ellis Island. It seemed as if we had waited for years for this trip (and in some ways we had) and the 5th grade hallway bubbled with excitement.

Many of us arrived early! This was a major accomplishment since most of us love to sleep, but the anticipation gave us all the motivation we needed. Squeak, boom, slam - lockers quickly opening and closing could be heard alongside squeals and laughter.

Mrs. T. rounded the corner, and at first we could see her usual smiling eyes. "All right, all right," she said in her trying to be stern but loving us too much voice. She added, "let's get to our homerooms so we can get this show on the road!"

This was the last normal moment of that day...

All of a sudden, the classroom phone rang, and Mrs. T dipped inside to answer it. Her eyes went from smiling to squinting to opened wide to rolling. We knew something wasn't right.

Writers, one of the things we learned is that sometimes writers start their stories with a setting lead. So let's try that in our class text about the class trip gone wrong.

← Consistent language

Take a moment to think about the setting and then turn and talk to share what you think we can add. Remember, we can include time, the weather, and a description of place in a setting lead. (Teacher pauses.) *Now turn and talk.* (Teacher listens to students as they turn and talk.)

← Verbal annotation

I heard you share so many ways we could begin our piece. Hal and Mika said . . . and Victoria and Nevea said . . . . What do you think about those possibilities? I'm going to add a few setting leads to our story,

← Consistent language

so we can choose the one that works best with the rest of our story. Writers, did you

← Reiterate the steps

see how we brainstormed different setting leads and added a few options to see which one works best?

← Consistent language

- Writerly life components such as writing habits or process skills. Teaching certain stages of the writing process—rehearsal, drafting, and revision.
- Craft techniques. If the craft technique is new to the writer, shared practice gives students the opportunity to actively try something with their peers and teacher. (See pages 71–72 for specific ideas.)

- A collective piece of class writing based on a shared experience (e.g., class trip, funny class incident, guest speaker)
- Chart paper, paper with document camera, or other projection device such as a SMART or Promethean Board

Video 4.3 Shared Writing

Facilitate a Shared Inquiry

With the shared inquiry method of demonstration, teacher and students alike are colearners, inquiring and discovering together. Students work with you to investigate how something is done and together you discover an idea, method, process, strategy, or set of craft moves. We might put up a great piece of writing and ask students to help us notice and name the craft or process moves the author makes so they can try these same moves in their writing.

Example: Shared Inquiry

Let's say we want to teach students to build writing stamina. When teaching using the shared inquiry method, we would investigate how one student worked on building writing stamina.

What I Might Say

Writers, let's look at Lauren's writing together. Do you notice how Lauren was writing shorter entries a few weeks ago but is writing longer entries now? Lauren has been working on her writing stamina because she wants to be able to write for longer periods of time. Let's take a moment to notice what Lauren is doing to build writing stamina. Then we'll turn and talk about what we notice. (Students turn and talk.) *Tanya and Eli were noticing that Lauren started skipping lines in some of her entries, and Ravi and Tom were noticing that Lauren was using a goal-setting X on her longer entries. What do we think about that? What can we call those moves?* (Students discuss what they noticed and name the moves.) *Did you see how Lauren used two strategies, skip lines and write to the X, to build her writing stamina?*

Consistent language

Verbal annotation

Consistent language

Verbal annotation

Reiterate the steps

Consistent language

- Writerly life components. Writing habits and process skills such as varying topic choice, generating writing ideas, and building writing stamina are well-matched to the shared inquiry model. Process skills, including rehearsing and revising writing are also a powerful match to the shared inquiry approach. By noticing an example, especially an example from a peer, and naming what they see, writers own the model in very specific learner-directed ways. (See pages 67–68 for specific ideas.)

- Genre elements. Uncover elements of a genre that you want your students to emulate by putting them in the driver's seat. Allow students to discover elements of a genre through shared inquiry.

NARRATIVE WRITING

- Create an architecture to the piece such as structuring it in chronological order or using time elements such as flashback or flashforward

- Utilize motifs of the genre such as a red herring in a mystery or magic and character archetypes in fantasy

- Include and perfect story elements such as setting, character, plot, and problem/solution

- Explore and choose a point of view through which the story is told

- Establish a lesson/theme/message and provide the reader with this big idea through characterization, craft, and plot

INFORMATIONAL WRITING

- Create an architecture to the piece such as structuring it as a main idea with supporting information, a chronological text, a question with a series of answers, or a problem with various solutions

- Consider the specific form of the text and how that impacts the reader: picture book, chapter book, how-to text, or short text such as an article or blog post

- Convey information with graphics such as pictures, captions, sidebars, maps, diagrams, zoom boxes, and other features

- Consider the tone that is used in the text, including whether it is a teaching tone, authoritative tone, or friendly peer-to-peer tone

OPINION/ARGUMENT WRITING

- Create an architecture to the piece such as structuring it as a journey-of-thought essay or a more academic reasons-and-evidence piece

- Think about the overall structure of thesis, body, and conclusion with transitions

- Be intentional about tone—persuasive or argumentative

- Try persuasive techniques such as offering different facts, quoting experts, and using powerful language and anecdotes

(continued)

POETRY

- Create an architecture to the piece such as structuring it as a free-verse or formed (haiku, limerick, concrete) poem
- Use stanzas, white space, and line breaks
- Try literary techniques such as sensory images, alliteration, assonance, rhyme, rhythm, and figurative language
- Consider the tone and mood of the piece

Craft techniques: When you allow learners to notice and name the craft, in writing, student ownership and usage is immediate. Learners become more active versus passive, and our diverse array of learners are highly engaged. (See pages 71–72 for specific ideas.)

Tools You Need

- A piece of writing to notice and dissect
- A chart for noticing and naming displayed on chart paper or a projection device such as a SMART or Promethean Board

Video 4.4 Shared Inquiry

Chapter 5

The Active Engagement

EVEN IF THE TEACHING IS clear, brief, and engaging, it will not necessarily lead to student understanding. Understanding comes when students have the opportunity, even briefly, to try out what you have just taught. This part of the minilesson is called active engagement and it is exactly that—an opportunity for students to engage with the teaching point by actively trying it in a piece of writing.

Students can try out the teaching point in one of two ways:

> ## with a teacher-provided writing model

> ## with their own writing

Both have the same purpose—to actively engage students—but they differ in their approach and proximity to the writer's work.

Using the Model from the Teaching

Actively engaging students with the model text used in the teaching is more secure and more easily managed. You know that students can apply the teaching point right away because the text and context are controlled. Asking students to try the teaching point with the demonstration text will work regardless of the method you used (i.e., teacher model, mentor text, shared writing, shared inquiry). Let's say you just taught writers to include inside story—their thoughts and feelings—in their narrative:

> **66**
>
> Teachers can answer children's questions only if they know the writing process inside and out. They know it from the inside because they work at their own writing; they know it from the outside because they are acquainted with research that shows what happens when people write.
>
> **Donald Graves (1983)**

Teacher Model

If you modeled your teaching point by writing in front of your students (**teacher model**), ask students to identify another place where you can add thoughts and feelings to your writing. Ask for suggestions on what you might add. It is helpful to choose a topic that is a shared experience or a simple story that students can relate to. *Writers, now it is your turn. Can you find another part where I can add thoughts or feelings? What can I add? Turn and talk to your partner about a place where I can add internal thinking or my feelings.*

Mentor Text

If you used a **mentor text,** ask students to notice thoughts and feelings in another place in the text. *Writers, now it is your turn. We already noticed that Ezra Jack Keats adds internal thinking and feelings throughout the text,* Peter's Chair. *I'm going to read another part and ask you to notice when he adds thoughts and feelings.* (Teacher reads the passage.) *Turn and talk to your partner and name what part you noticed and share why you think he added that thought or feeling.*

Shared Writing

If your teaching demonstration was through **shared writing**, the teaching and active engagement happen together, and students have been actively engaged in cocreating a shared text. Continue that work but hand over the reins a bit more. *Writers, now it is your turn to create the next part, but let's be sure to include elements of inside story, specifically internal thinking and feelings. Turn and talk to your partner ("write in the air") and envision how we can add thoughts and feelings to our shared writing piece.* (Teacher listens in to students' responses; adds student ideas to the text.)

Consistent language

Inclusive Practices to Support Every Writer

One instructional strategy we use during the active engagement part of the minilesson is the turn-and-talk. During a turn-and-talk, students have a focused chat with a peer. They might notice and discuss craft in the mentor text or talk about how they'll try the teaching point in their own writing. During turn-and-talks think about:

1 Establishing long-term partnerships (for the unit, quarter, or any other length of time that will meet the needs of your students). This will avoid a long transition to the active engagement and enable you to pair students for success. In addition, consider naming your partners (partner A and partner B; peanut butter and jelly) so you can help scaffold the active engagement. For example, you might have your students who benefit from a direct peer model be partner B. Ask partner A to share first, thus allowing partner B to benefit from the model.

2 Encouraging students to speak in their home/native language, or use both their native language and English. This allows all students to be active and engaged during this part of the minilesson.

3 Trios, not just partners. For more vulnerable learners, two strong peer mentors can offer the support and modeling they need. We know that with language acquisition, receptive language comes before expressive. Being part of a trio gives students time to watch and listen before jumping in.

Shared Inquiry

If your demonstration was through **shared inquiry**, students have been actively engaging in and inquiring in a shared text or experience. Continue that work here, but hand over the reins a bit more. *Writers, we have just unpacked the first part of Luke's piece to find evidence of how he is incorporating elements other than the plot. We named this "what we think about what is happening." So far we found that he includes internal thinking and his feelings at important or pivotal parts. Let's move on to the next part, noticing what Luke is doing and naming it using the language we have created.*

Luke's Writing

After my mom closed my bedroom door I sat frozen on my bed. "Could this really be happening to Tucker? He is only 9 years old," I thought to myself. — *Inside Story - Internal Thinking*

Inside Story - Showing NOT Telling Feelings — After being frozen like a statue, I jumped off my bed. I paced around my room, around and around, in circles. Tears were forming in my eyes.

Inside Story - Internal Thinking — Visions of Tucker and I ran through my mind. Tucker and I playing fetch, Tucker and I watching movies, Tucker and I sharing a bowl of ice cream. "I won't let this happen. I can't let this happen," played in my mind just like the memories.

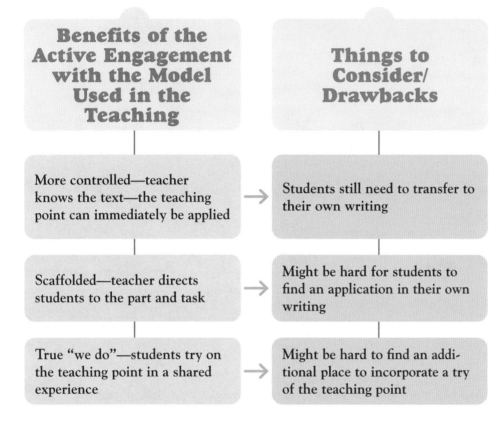

Benefits of the Active Engagement with the Model Used in the Teaching	Things to Consider/ Drawbacks
More controlled—teacher knows the text—the teaching point can immediately be applied	→ Students still need to transfer to their own writing
Scaffolded—teacher directs students to the part and task	→ Might be hard for students to find an application in their own writing
True "we do"—students try on the teaching point in a shared experience	→ Might be hard to find an additional place to incorporate a try of the teaching point

Video 5.1 Active Engagement with the Model Used in the Teaching Portion

It is helpful to choose a topic that is a shared experience or a simple story that students can relate to.

Using Students' Own Writing

Another way to actively engage students is to have them try the teaching point with their own writing. This method can feel a bit riskier because each student is working with different content, but it's effective because of its direct proximity to the students' ongoing work. During the active engagement portion of the minilesson, students try the teaching point in their independent writing. This works particularly well when you teach students something new, and know it's a strategy they can use immediately. Once again, students can try on this strategy, regardless of the method of demonstration.

Teacher Model

If you modeled this in your own writing (**teacher model**), allow students to try this in their writing. *Writers, now it is your turn. Find a part where you can add inside story, or thoughts and feelings, to your writing. Use the steps that I did: find a part; decide whether you want to add a thought or a feeling. (Teacher pauses as students find a place.) Turn and talk to your partner about a place where you can add inside story. Write in the air, sharing with your partner what you could write.*

Consistent language

Aditya's Try-it

"She's soft, and pretty, and always there for me," I thought.

(After the part where she drives away)

I stomped my feet and clenched my hands.

(Instead of saying I was mad)

Mentor Text

If your demonstration was in a **mentor text**, allow students the opportunity to insert thoughts and feelings in their writing. *Writers, now it is your turn. Ezra Jack Keats adds internal thinking and feelings throughout the text* Peter's Chair. *You can do this too! Find a part where you can add thoughts and feelings to your writing. Use the steps that we inferred Ezra used: find a part; decide whether you want to add a thought or a feeling; add. Jot down what you can add to your piece.*

Shared Practice

If your demonstration was via a **shared practice** using shared writing, students have been actively engaging in the co-creating of a shared text. Continue that work here, but hand the reins over to their writing. *Writers, we just practiced adding thoughts and feelings to our class text, and now it is your turn. Find a part where you can add thoughts and feelings to your writing. Use the steps that we did: find a part; decide whether you want to add a thought or a feeling; add. Once you find a part, turn to your partner and write in the air, saying aloud what you will add to your piece.*

Shared Inquiry

If your demonstration was via **shared inquiry,** students have been actively engaging and inquiring in a shared text or experience. Continue that work here, but hand the reins over to their writing. *Writers, we have just unpacked the first part of Luke's piece to find evidence of how he is incorporating elements other than the plot. We named this "what we think a writer is doing and why." So far we found that he includes internal thinking and his feelings at important or pivotal parts, such as before or after an interaction with another character. Now it is your turn. Find a part where you can add thoughts and feelings to your writing. Use the steps that Luke did: find a part; decide whether you want to add your thoughts, or a feeling; add. Once you find a part, turn to your partner and write in the air, saying aloud what you will add to your piece.*

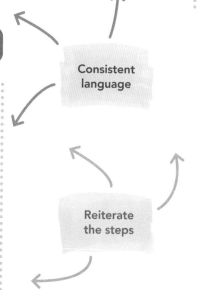

Consistent language

Reiterate the steps

Tip

When planning minilessons, it's important to remember that the purpose of active engagement is to provide students with a short time to try out the new strategy that was just taught. Students rarely write during active engagement (they might do a quick jot). Instead, they are thinking, planning, turning and talking, and writing in the air. For example, if you just taught students to begin a narrative by describing the setting, students should not begin drafting their setting lead in their notebooks as they sit on the carpet. So this tip is really a warning: don't let active engagement turn into independent practice!

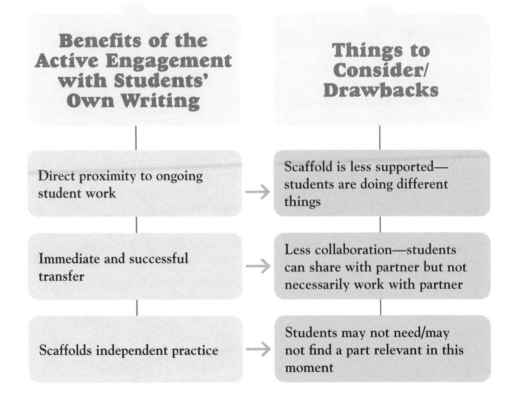

Benefits of the Active Engagement with Students' Own Writing	Things to Consider/ Drawbacks
Direct proximity to ongoing student work	Scaffold is less supported—students are doing different things
Immediate and successful transfer	Less collaboration—students can share with partner but not necessarily work with partner
Scaffolds independent practice	Students may not need/may not find a part relevant in this moment

Video 5.2 Active Engagement with Students Using Their Own Writing

A Teacher's Guide to Writing Workshop Minilessons

Establish long-term partnerships (for the unit, quarter, or any other length of time that will meet the needs of your students). This will avoid a long transition to the active engagement and enable you to pair students for success.

Chapter 6

The Link

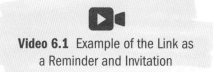

Video 6.1 Example of the Link as a Reminder and Invitation

AS WE SAY TO WRITERS, the end is just as important as the beginning. This is just as true for minilessons as it is for writing. The last part of the minilesson, the link, is your opportunity to leave writers with clarity and a plan. We often think of this part of the minilesson as a bookend to the first part of the mini-lesson, because it is similar in purpose, tone, and length. The language we use in the link wraps up the lesson and invites students to try the work that we just explored in the connection, teaching, and active engagement.

End Your Lesson with a Reminder and an Invitation

You want to use language that contextualizes and reminds students of the teaching point but does not make the independent practice that follows *only* about what has been taught. Today's teaching point needs to fit inside of the ongoing work of writers and writing workshop. It should serve as an invitation for how a student can spend *part* of the independent practice time. For example: *Today as you go off to write, remember that one way writers stretch out the important parts of their personal narrative is to include inside story—what you are thinking and feeling. We've talked about other ways to revise your writing and stretch out the important parts of a personal narrative and we've been adding that to our chart. This is one more strategy to add to your writing toolbox as you make a plan for writing.*

Tip

As you plan your minilessons, be sure the language you use in your link sounds like an invitation, not an assignment. For example, a link that is inviting might sound something like *Today as you go off to write, remember that one way writers _____ is to _____. We've talked about other ways to _____. This is one more strategy to add to your writing toolbox.* A link that sounds like an assignment might sound something like *Today you will spend your time adding _____ to your drafts. It's important to make sure you do this as it will make your piece more interesting.* The goal of the minilesson isn't to micromanage the writing time and assign students work for the day. Students may spend part of the writing time working on something related to the teaching point but will also have other plans for the writing time.

You want to use language that contextualizes and reminds students of the teaching point but does not make the independent practice that follows *only* about what has been taught.

End Your Lesson with a Plan

Before students begin independent writing time, help them make a plan for the day. The plan should consider the minilesson, but more importantly, consider what the writer needs to be working on today. You will then add: *Let's make that plan for today's writing workshop. Think about what we have just learned about adding thoughts and feelings as you make a plan for how you will spend your writing time today.*

You can ask writers to create a plan in one of the following ways:

> **"**
>
> **The language that teachers (and their students) use in a classroom is a big deal.**
>
> **Peter Johnston (2004)**

1

Turn and talk to a writing partner.

Turn and talk to your writing partner. Share your plan for today.

2

Make a plan and jot it down.

Think about your writing plan. Jot the plan down on a sticky note.

3

Think of a plan and quickly report it on a status of the class (Atwell 1998) **chart.**

Take a look at the options for how we will start the writing time. Jot your name on a sticky note. Put your name in the column that indicates your plan for how you will begin today.

As students create their writing plans, notice and note their intentions for the day, and then send them off to write. This ensures that the link truly connects the writer to an actionable plan. It also helps you get a sense of what writers will be doing during today's writing time. You can send them off in one of three ways:

1
In partnerships

As partners are sharing their writing plans, we want to quickly listen in, and then send them off to write. *Writers, share today's plan with your partner. Your plan may be connected to the minilesson, or your plan may be connected to what you have been working on as a writer. When you have shared your plan and feel ready, go off to write.*

2
One by one

Another instructional strategy is to listen to partners as they are sharing their plans, or quickly look at their jots, and then tap writers, one by one, or invite writers to decide for themselves, when they are ready to go off.

3
By small group

After writers jot or partners turn and talk, we can get a quick status of the class and send writers off in a staggered way, by group, based on the plan. *Writers, jot your name on a sticky note.* (Pause.) *Thumbs up if you are going to start the writing time by working to insert character internal thinking. Add your sticky note to that column in the chart and then head off to write. Thumbs up if you are going to start the writing time by rereading your writing and working on adding dialogue to scenes. Add your sticky note . . .*

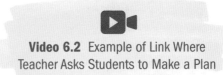
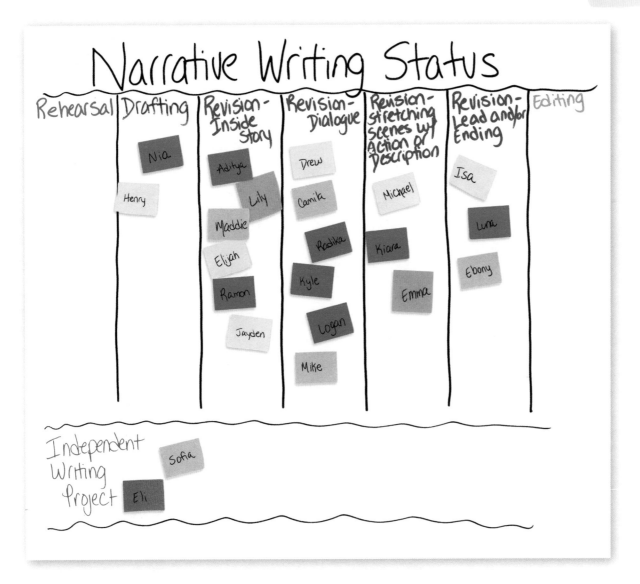

Narrative Writing Status

Rehearsal	Drafting	Revision-Inside Story	Revision-Dialogue	Revision-Stretching scenes w/ Action or Description	Revision-Lead and/or Ending	Editing

Nia

Henry

Aditya

Lily

Maddie

Elijah

Ramon

Jayden

Drew

Camila

Radika

Kyle

Logan

Mike

Michael

Kiara

Emma

Isa

Luna

E'bony

Independent Writing Project

Sofia

Eli

Support Writers as They Transition to Writing Time

Video 6.3 Example of Students Staying on the Carpet and Working with the Teacher

If students need further clarification, invite them to stay with you for another minute or two. So, after students have a plan, you might add: *If you are not sure what your plan is, stay with me in our meeting area for another minute so we can make a plan together.* In this instance, you can have a quick individual or group conference to ensure that the lesson is clear and that you provide enough support for all students. Three scenarios tend to happen:

1

Students have a question they need clarification on.

Begin by asking students if they have questions or by asking students what their plan is. This will enable you to clarify and quickly send off.

2

Students have a plan, but need help getting started.

They might share thoughts such as: "I am not sure what idea on my list to write about." "I know what inside story is, but I am not sure where to put that in my piece." Or even "I know where I want to add to my piece, but I am not sure what to write." In those instances, conduct quick coaching conferences where students who are there may even jump into the coaching as a way to support others and themselves.

3

Students do not understand the teaching point.

If this is the case, consider conducting a small-group lesson that is a minilesson do-over (Vitale-Reilly 2017). In this instance, you want to reteach the minilesson quickly, but you will want to do something different. More of the same has a very low ceiling and impact on learners. For example, if you used a text to model the minilesson, consider a shared practice through shared writing. This change in methodology will be more likely to support the learners, as shared writing incorporates students' active engagement from the start.

Inclusive Practices to Support Every Writer

If students have a question or need help getting started, consider peer collaboration. A peer can answer a question, help brainstorm, rehearse an idea in a learner's native language, or can be a sounding board to listen and provide feedback. In addition, a peer can show the writer who needs support what they did to get started. Consider providing sentence stems to support the talk and build the academic vocabulary around writing. Or, provide writers with annotated task/craft cards to complement the conversation. Supporting by showing a peer's work is a powerful practice that stands on the shoulders of the "just like me" dynamic. This other writer is just like me—a writer in my class who had the same challenge and solved it!

Supporting by showing a peer's work is a powerful practice that stands on the shoulders of the "just like me" dynamic. This other writer is just like me—a writer in my class who had the same challenge and solved it!

Chapter 7

How Does It All Come Together?

LET'S SEE HOW ALL THE parts of the minilesson come together . . .

Sample Minilesson

CONNECTION

Writers, we have spent the last couple of weeks writing personal narratives. We've learned how to find moments that matter and stretch out the most important parts by including specific actions. (Teacher pauses.) We can also stretch out the important parts of our writing in another way—by including the inside story. The inside story is what is inside of you—your internal thinking and feelings. So today I am going to teach you how to include inside story into your personal narratives by adding it into my story about Rosco.

TEACHING

Writers, my story includes what happened when I took Rosco to the trainer for the first time, but it is missing the inside story: my internal thinking and feelings. (Teacher points to head and heart when she says "thinking" and "feeling.") During the part where we get out of the car and I hand the leash over to Linnea, I am going to add inside story: my internal thinking. ". . . slowly I walked over to Linnea. Questions ran through my mind: 'Am I really going to do this? Should I be doing this?' I handed her the leash hesitantly and could swear he looked back at me to say goodbye. 'I hope she takes care of him and remembers he likes a long pet and pat on the head before he goes to sleep,' I thought to myself." Did you notice how I (teacher lists the steps in the process using her fingers to demonstrate each step) first found a part where I can add inside story? And then I decided whether I was adding internal thinking or what I was feeling. I then added it to my piece. You will want to do this in your piece when you find places where you can add inside story.

Video 7.1 Sample Minilesson 1

ACTIVE ENGAGEMENT

Writers, now it is your turn. Find a part where you can add inside story, or thoughts and feelings, to your writing. Use the steps that I did: find a part; decide whether you want to add a thought or a feeling. (Teacher pauses as students find a place.) Turn and talk to your partner about a place where you can add inside story. Write in the air, sharing with your partner what you could write.

LINK

Today as you go off to write, remember that one way writers stretch out the important parts of their personal narrative is to include inside story—what you are thinking and feeling. We've talked about other ways to revise your writing and stretch out the important parts of a personal narrative and we've been adding that to our chart. This is one more strategy to add to your writing toolbox as you make a plan for writing.

Video 7.2 Sample Minilesson 2

Whether you are teaching in a hybrid or remote learning model, incorporating some remote minilessons allows you to carve out more time to support learners.

Inclusive Practices to Support Every Writer

There are many things to consider in addition to what to teach and how to teach it; you will also want to consider your students' needs. One way to address the needs of emergent bilinguals is to pay attention to the ways that they can achieve maximum understanding of the language and concepts taught in a minilesson. *Comprehensible input* (Krashen 1982) is a term that means that all students can access and understand what is being taught in a lesson. Students may not have all the necessary background or conceptual knowledge, nor may they understand all the words spoken. However, if we teach with comprehensible input in mind, all learners derive meaning from the minilesson. Consider the following suggestions:

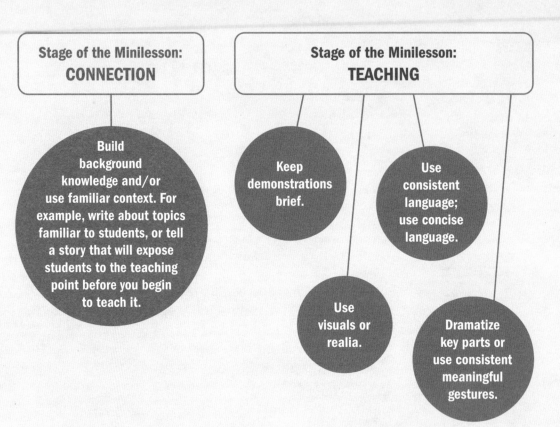

Stage of the Minilesson: **CONNECTION**

Build background knowledge and/or use familiar context. For example, write about topics familiar to students, or tell a story that will expose students to the teaching point before you begin to teach it.

Stage of the Minilesson: **TEACHING**

Keep demonstrations brief.

Use consistent language; use concise language.

Use visuals or realia.

Dramatize key parts or use consistent meaningful gestures.

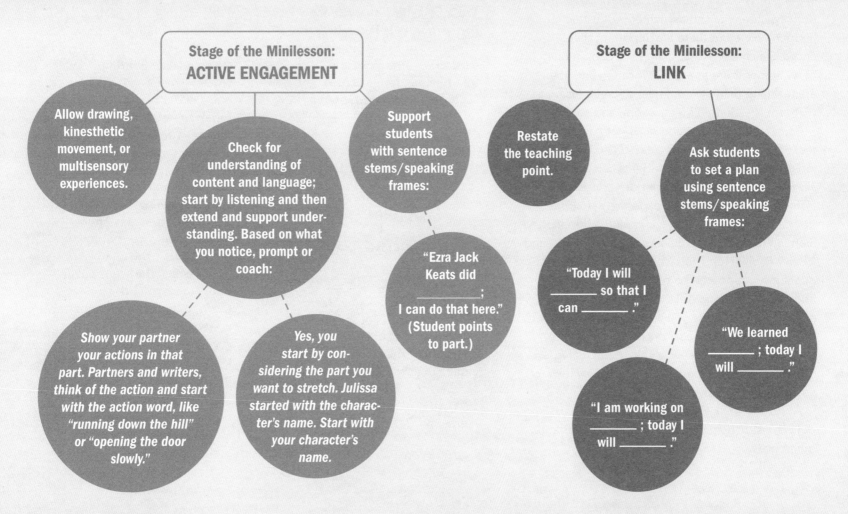

Stage of the Minilesson: ACTIVE ENGAGEMENT

Allow drawing, kinesthetic movement, or multisensory experiences.

Check for understanding of content and language; start by listening and then extend and support understanding. Based on what you notice, prompt or coach:

Support students with sentence stems/speaking frames:

Show your partner your actions in that part. Partners and writers, think of the action and start with the action word, like "running down the hill" or "opening the door slowly."

Yes, you start by considering the part you want to stretch. Julissa started with the character's name. Start with your character's name.

"Ezra Jack Keats did _____; I can do that here." (Student points to part.)

Stage of the Minilesson: LINK

Restate the teaching point.

Ask students to set a plan using sentence stems/speaking frames:

"Today I will _____ so that I can _____ ."

"We learned _____ ; today I will _____ ."

"I am working on _____ ; today I will _____ ."

Delivering Minilessons in Different Instructional Settings

There are three ways to deliver minilessons—in person, synchronously, or asynchronously. Both synchronous and asynchronous instruction happen online but there are important differences. Synchronous instruction happens in real time. Students are at another location and you are teaching them live but over a screen (using a platform like Google Meet, Zoom, and so on).

Asynchronous instruction does not happen in real time. The teacher has created a video recording of the minilesson and students can access the video any time. When we consider asynchronous instruction, we can borrow expertise and ideas from the educators who have implemented flipped learning (Bergmann and Sams 2012; Johansen and Cherry-Paul 2016). Their work, creating videos of direct instruction, can be offered to students for homework or during class independently or in a small group. Whether you are teaching in a hybrid or remote learning model, incorporating some asynchronous minilessons allows you to carve out more time to support learners as they look to navigate this somewhat challenging terrain.

When you think about the different ways to deliver instruction, consider both similarities and differences.

Similarities Across Instructional Settings

The Structure of the Minilesson

We fully believe that the four-part structure is best practice regardless of the setting. Each part serves a purpose and is intentionally implemented according to that purpose.

Instructional Tools

Although you may display or share differently in different settings, the tools you use for writing minilessons stay the same: models of writing (teacher, text, student), anchor charts and other visual supports, paper choices that allow teachers to model in the medium that matches the learners and the lesson.

Teaching Points

Although a unit's pacing, sequence of minilessons, or scope of skills may be altered to accommodate hybrid or remote teaching, a specific teaching point does not have to be removed or altered due to the setting. You want to make sure that you create curriculum that is most responsive to students, and that includes being responsive to teaching in any context. Therefore, you may choose to restructure your units of study so that the number of minilessons, the sequence of minilessons, and the time it takes to implement the unit are revised to match the setting or scenario. The actual teaching points—what we teach students about writing and writers—does not change.

Differences Across Instructional Settings

Tighter Timing

As a general rule of thumb, in-person minilessons are ten to fifteen minutes long. When minilessons are delivered on a screen, you want to tighten your timing and adhere to online learning recommendations. Why? One reason is that the screen acts as an affective filter (Krashen 1982). An affective filter is a barrier, emotional or otherwise, that impedes learning. A screen can be an affective filter for some students, and one way to remove this barrier is to shorten the time a student is learning on a screen. A synchronous minilesson should be 3–5 minutes shorter than an in-person minilesson. For example, if your in-person minilesson usually lasts twelve minutes, your synchronous minilesson should last 7–10 minutes. Krashen's research impacts asynchronous minilessons even more. During asynchronous learning, students do not have the benefit of the teacher or their peers, and teachers do not have the ability to check for understanding and read the "room" (or screen). According to online course research, *How Video Production Affects Student Engagement* by Philip Guo, Juho Kim, and Rob Rubin (2013), videos should be no longer than six minutes.

Tools: Medium and Student Access

Although you have access to the same tools as when you teach in person, you may need to change how you use and display the tools to students. If, in an in-person lesson, I displayed the anchor chart on a piece of chart paper on an easel or board, I might want to think about the access students would have to that tool in an online setting. I may choose to put the anchor chart in Google Classroom or another learning management system, or put the anchor chart in Google Slides that are displayed as I share my screen during the appropriate parts of the minilesson. I can also choose to hold up the anchor chart in front of my camera. This last option only allows students to view the chart while I'm teaching, so I want to make sure students can access the chart digitally at any time.

continues

Nuances in the Delivery of the Minilesson

After much trial and error, we firmly landed on the belief that the minilesson structure remains the same in all synchronous settings (in person or on screen). In the asynchronous setting (prerecorded writing minilesson videos) the teacher can use the same structure or combine the last two stages—the active engagement and the link. You'll want to base your decision on your learners and what they need. What you do in the connection, teaching, and active engagement is altered in an online setting, because the students aren't physically in front of you. Even the link is different. If students aren't literally "going off" to write in a brick-and-mortar classroom, you'll want to connect the teaching to independent practice in a way that matches the setting. Let's see what kind of changes you might make to your minilesson based on the setting.

You want to make sure that you create curriculum that is most responsive to students, and that includes being responsive to teaching in any context.

In an in-person minilesson, here's how it all comes together:

In-Person Minilesson

Connection

Connect to and engage students with a recap of learning or quick story; *announce the teaching point.*

·········· Sample Language ··········

We have been . . . Another way to . . . So today I am going to teach you . . .

Teaching

Model *one teaching* point; *demonstrate* as much as you can.

·········· Sample Language ··········

Watch me as I . . . Did you see how I . . .

Active Engagement

Students *try out* teaching point.

·········· Sample Language ··········

Now it is your turn to try. Turn to your partner OR find a place in your writing where you can try OR envision how you will . . .

Link

Recap teaching; connect to ongoing work.

·········· Sample Language ··········

We have learned how to . . . Today make a plan for how you are going to . . .

In virtual synchronous minilessons, here's how it comes together:

Virtual Synchronous Minilesson

Connection

Social-emotional welcome (SEL); connect to and engage students with a recap of learning or quick story; *announce the teaching point.*

· · · · · · · · · · · · · · · Sample Language · · · · · · · · · · · · · · ·

Welcome, Wildcats! Let's begin with our quick morning hello. We are now ready to learn. I was working with Lexi, and we discovered . . . So today I am going to teach you . . .

Take time to acknowledge students.

Teaching

Quickly model one teaching point in virtual format; *demonstrate* as much as you can.

· · · · · · · · · · · · · Sample Language · · · · · · · · · · · · ·

Watch me as I . . . Did you see how I . . . ?

We recommend a platform that allows you to write on a screen instead of paper so students can see you compose.

Active Engagement

Ask students to *try out* the teaching point with a quick try conducive to your virtual setting or by envisioning doing what you just taught.

················ Sample Language ················

Now it is your turn to try. **Talk to your partner in the breakout room . . .** OR *Take a look at your writing and find a place where you can try this today. Put your thumb up when you have envisioned how this could go.*

Breakout rooms are a great option if you know how to use them. Another good option is to ask students to envision the work with an added tactile element. Ask students to point to a spot in their writing and envision what they'll work on. Finally, students give a nonverbal signal to demonstrate they have completed the active engagement.

Link

Remind students of what you just taught. *Send them off* to work. *Let them know* how you will *check in*/provide *feedback.*

················ Sample Language ················

We have learned how to . . . Now it is time to go off and work on . . . OR *Chat your plan in the chat box and go off to write.* OR *Whisper out what your plan is today and go off and write. I will check in with you in breakout rooms* OR *on your Google doc,* OR *when you are back in school tomorrow . . . I can't wait to see your . . .*

The planning should match the synchronous setting—chatting in the chat box for older writers and whispering out for our more emergent learners.

There are synchronous (in a breakout room or in-person on another day) and asynchronous (on a doc, not in real time) options for the check-ins so that these match the setting but also provide flexibility to teacher and students alike.

In virtual asynchronous minilessons there are two options. The first option merges active engagement and the link:

Virtual Asynchronous Minilesson · Option 1

Connection

Social-emotional welcome; connect to/engage students by a recap of learning or quick story; *announce the teaching point.*

········· **Sample Language** ·········

Welcome, writers! I am excited to continue our unit together and want us to begin with a shared read of our poem just like we do in the classroom. Join me! We are now ready to learn. We have been . . . Another way to . . . So today I am going to teach you . . .

Here I'm asking students to "join in" on what is typically an in-person routine.

Teaching

Quickly model one teaching point in virtual format; *demonstrate* as much as you can.

········· **Sample Language** ·········

Watch me as I . . . Did you see how I . . . ?

Your face should be visible alongside the model just as it would be in person. For example, you may be writing in a Google doc while filming in Screencastify. Even though this is a video, the instruction is still in a minilesson format, and the teach part of the minilesson includes demonstration of the teaching point.

Link

Remind students of what you just taught. **Ask them** to envision doing it. **Send them off** to work. **Let them know** how you will **check in**/provide feedback.

························ **Sample Language** ························

We have learned how to . . . Now it is your turn to try. Think about how you will . . . today. Pause for 3–5 seconds. I will check in with you . . . (in . . . , in breakout rooms, on your doc, in Seesaw, during our scheduled small-group session). I can't wait to see you . . .

The active practice and link are combined to accommodate the online asynchronous setting. Send students off in a way that matches the setting. When students have a scheduled time for feedback, collaboration, and synchronous learning, they approach their independent writing with purpose. In addition, keep a social-emotional connection to students by ending with how and where you will be together again.

> **"**
>
> When we flipped some of our lessons, we covered more content. We had more time for individualized instruction and conferences.
>
> **Dana Johansen and
> Sonja Cherry-Paul (2016)**

How Does It All Come Together?

The second virtual asynchronous minilessons option uses all parts of the mini-lesson but moves along quickly.

Virtual Asynchronous Minilesson · Option 2

Connection

SEL welcome; connect to/engage students by a recap of learning or quick story; *announce the teaching point.*

············· Sample Language ·············

Welcome writers! I am excited to continue our unit together and want us to begin with a shared read of our poem just like we do in the classroom. Join me! We are now ready to learn. We have been . . . Another way to . . . So today I am going to teach you . . .

I take about a half minute to virtually ask students to "join in" on what is typically an in-person routine.

Teaching

Quickly model one teaching point in virtual format; *demonstrate* as much as you can.

············· Sample Language ·············

Watch me as I . . . Did you see how I . . . ?

Demonstration is still the method of teaching. We do not want to create slides and voice-over directions. Remember that your face should be visible alongside the model.

Active Engagement

Students **actively engage** with the teaching point by doing a quick exercise conducive to the virtual setting.

········ **Sample Language** ········

Now it is your turn to think about . . . Is there a place where you can try this in your writing? Quickly find that place, and while you are pointing to that place, use your finger to name the steps you will take to do that. OR, Writers, now it is your turn to think about this work. Is there a place where you can try this in your writing? Pause for 5 seconds. Point to that place and envision how this work will go. Picture in your mind what you will write and how you will say it. Pause for another 10 seconds or so.

I can actively engage students in two ways: find and talk out the steps or find and envision the what and the how. Each is timely and appropriate in an asynchronous setting as they do not require collaboration or teacher input.

I am pausing quickly so students can give it a try. I am not asking students to talk to another person (this may be hard for many students in a home setting), pause the video, or create something (this is too time-consuming, and I am not available to offer feedback).

Link

Remind students of what you just taught. **Send them off** to work. **Let them know** how you will **check in/** provide **feedback**.

········ **Sample Language** ········

Now it is time to go off and work on . . . I will check in with you . . . (in breakout rooms, on your doc, in Seesaw, during our scheduled small group for tomorrow). I can't wait to see your . . .

Video 7.3
Sample Minilesson—Asynchronous

Chapter 8

Match Your Lessons to Your Students' Needs

AS WRITING TEACHERS, WE WANT to have lessons in mind based on what we know about writing and what we learn about the students in front of us. This is true even if you use a district-created curriculum, a mandated curriculum based on state standards, or a curricular resource. Assessment is what helps us match our lessons to meet the needs of students. As students write, you will want to assess their work and allow what you learn to inform your minilessons. There are a few ways to do that.

> **"**
>
> The research is clear that the one factor that matters more than anything in determining whether students' levels of achievement accelerate is the quality of your teaching. You need to teach responsively.
>
> **Lucy Calkins (2013)**

Kidwatching

We assess students constantly. From the moment they arrive at school, to the moment they get on the bus to go home, we make a thousand small observations about each child and the group. These observations influence how we run our classroom, interact with students, and teach. The practice of "watching kids with a knowledgeable head" (9) or kidwatching (Owocki and Goodman 2002) is a great way to inform your writing instruction.

It helps to observe your students at all phases of the writing workshop to glean information about their habits and process. You will want to notice things like who leaves the carpet and immediately gets started writing and who takes a long time to get going. Who seeks out a writing partner to get feedback during writing? Who keeps a mentor text next to them as they write? What kinds of tools are students using as they write? All of these observations provide insight into students' habits and processes and provide material for future minilessons.

Here are some of the things you might observe and questions you can use to guide your observations.

Habits

Movement Before and After Minilesson

Who comes to the rug right away and who lingers behind? Who leaves the meeting area immediately and who takes a longer time to transition to independent writing? Who seeks out the extra support offered at the end of the minilesson?

Level of Social Interaction

Who seeks out a writing partner? Who prefers to work alone?

Use of Mentor Text

Who seeks out or refers to a mentor text while writing? Who keeps a text out and with them as they write?

Use of Charts in the Classroom

Who is referring to the charts in the classroom?

Tools

What kind of paper is a child choosing? Who is stapling additional pages to their books? Who is carrying a notebook around? How are students using their writer's notebook—as a tool utilizing all sections, or just as a collection container for writing?

Process

Rehearsal

How are writers collecting ideas? Who is using a previously generated idea chart? How are they researching for upcoming writing? What kind of planning techniques are writers using? Who is stuck and unable to generate an idea or generate writing for a chosen idea?

Drafting

Who's quickly getting words down on their paper? Who is using their notes from the rehearsal part of the process?

Revising

Who is using mentor texts? Who is seeking help from a partner or group? Who is using strategies from minilessons?

Editing

Who is using an editing checklist or chart? Who is seeking out peer support or signing up for a conference? What other tools are students using (e.g., dictionary, word wall, thesaurus, spell check)?

Publishing

Is anyone seeking out independent publishing projects? Who is adding illustrations to their work? Who is adding special pages such as a table of contents or an about the author page? Is anyone making a cover? What are students doing to consider the needs of their audience?

You will want to kidwatch throughout the year by occasionally taking a day off from conducting typical conferences. Instead, observe your group at work or conduct quick writing assessment conferences in which you observe writers and then sit down with them and probe deeper. This information is invaluable. It helps you plan minilessons that teach new procedures and strategies that make writing every day more productive for every child.

What I Notice a Student Doing	What I Think It Means	How This Impacts What I Teach
Several students ask to go to the bathroom each day directly after being dismissed from the minilesson.	This is one example of a writing avoidance behavior. I know this can be caused by: • not knowing what to write • not knowing how to get started • feeling overwhelmed by the blank page.	I'll revisit idea-generating strategies and see if this helps. If the behavior continues, I will consider other lessons on getting started and maintaining focus.
One student is squeezing words into a very crowded draft.	The student is revising and wants to add more details but there isn't enough room on the page.	Teach students to add things in using the "star" system. Put numbered stars where you want to add in text and write the additional text on a clean page (star 1, star 2, star 3, etc.). This ensures students have plenty of space to revise.
One student is jotting notes in the margins of a draft, leaving lots of lines between each note.	The student is making plans on the draft.	Ask the student to share with others how they make a plan by writing in the margins.

Kidwatching Chart

What I Notice a Student Doing	What I Think It Means	How This Impacts What I Teach in Minilessons
Several students ask to go to the bathroom each day directly after being dismissed from the minilesson.	This is one example of a writing avoidance behavior. I know this can be caused by: • not knowing what to write • not knowing how to get started • feeling overwhelmed by the blank page.	I'll revisit idea-generating strategies and see if this helps. If the behavior continues, I will consider other lessons on getting started and maintaining focus.

> " Your responsibility as a kid watcher is to allow children meaningful opportunities for writing that draw from their social and cultural experiences and to help them explore new possibilities. The most informative kind of evaluation occurs as children are engaged in learning experiences that they find personally and culturally meaningful.
>
> **Gretchen Owocki and Yetta Goodman (2002)**

Inclusive Practices to Support Every Writer

You want to ensure that when you plan minilessons, you do so with your students' strengths and differences in mind. One way to do that is to know your students well and to use what you know to specifically plan your instruction. Don Graves, father of the writing workshop, always inspired teachers to stand on the shoulders of a relationship with students by knowing at least ten things about a student before you teach them.

Knowing your students well includes knowing them as people and as learners. We believe that this includes three lenses: interests, habits, and previous experiences.

INTERESTS

Begin your year with interest inventories using a paper survey, Google Form, or another tech platform. Use your beginning-of-the-year conferences with students to talk about what you learned, or pair students up to interview each other. Tap into the hobbies, talents, and interests that motivate your students. *I was so excited to learn that you are an avid musician and that you have played the clarinet for six years! That is a lot of hard work and time to put into an activity. What have you learned about playing the clarinet that you think can help you as a writer?*

HABITS

Identify the habits your students already have as learners and tap into that. For example, if a student has a habit of packing their own backpack or choosing their own snack, name it and connect it to writing. *I know you are such a responsible student getting your materials/lunch ready for school the next day. Writers get ready too. You can jot a quick plan for tomorrow at the end of each writing workshop.*

EXPERIENCES

Use storytelling in your week and in your units. Storytelling is a great writing rehearsal strategy, but it is also a way to get to know the cultural and personal experiences of your students. These experiences can include previous school experiences for students new to your school or our country. You can then use these experiences in a strengths-based model. *I know that every summer when you visit your abuela you help her visit all of the older relatives. These experiences make great narrative pieces, or even argument pieces about ways to support older generations.*

Assessing the Group's Writing

In addition to observing your students as they work, you can also match your minilessons to your students' needs by examining their writing. Your students will be writing each day in connection with the current unit of study. It is beneficial to assess students' writing before, during, and after a unit so you can tailor your instruction to meet their ongoing needs. Here are some ways you might assess students throughout a unit:

Online Resource 8.2
Whole-Group Assessment Chart

Whole-Group Assessments

When

Before the unit

Type of Whole-Group Assessment

On demand (Calkins and colleagues 2013)

How

Ask students to write their best piece in one writing workshop session.

Benefits

When you assess students before a unit begins, it helps you tailor your instruction from the start. If you're using a curriculum resource, it gives you the opportunity to pick and choose the minilessons your students need; or if you are creating your own writing curriculum, it allows you to design minilessons tailored to the needs of your students.

Whole-Group Assessment Chart

Date	Type of Whole-Group Assessment	Student Needs/ Noticings	Possible Minilessons

continues

When

During the unit

How

As students write, make time to collect their writing folders and/or notebooks and assess their ongoing work. Try to do this several times during a unit. It is helpful to have criteria in mind as you assess. This might be a checklist, rubric, learning progression, or other assessment tool that will guide your observations.

Type of Whole-Group Assessment

Students' ongoing writing in folders or notebooks

Benefits

Collecting students' writing during a unit allows you to modify your instruction. As you read through their ongoing work, you can see whether they are understanding concepts you recently taught, and if not, plan more lessons on them. You will also see if they're ready to learn something new.

When

After the unit

How

Ask students to do another on demand piece of writing or gather their final piece to assess.

Type of Whole-Group Assessment

On demand or final piece

Benefits

Looking across students' final pieces will give you information about your teaching. What concepts did students master? What concepts are they still struggling with? You can then take this knowledge with you into future units.

Tip

When assessing students' writing during conferences or as a group, be sure to look for potential student mentor texts (Eickholdt 2015). Although you will typically be assessing students' writing needs, you will also want to look for strong examples. Perhaps many of your students are struggling to elaborate the most important part or heart of their story, but one student has nailed this technique. Invite that student to help you teach the minilesson and use their writing as the mentor text. Not only will it build that child's self-esteem, but it will convey to others that this technique is doable. Nothing is a more developmentally appropriate mentor text than a classmate's writing.

Using Conferences to Make Teaching Decisions

The hallmark of workshop teaching is individualized instruction. Conferring with students as they write enables you to individualize your teaching to meet every child's needs. Conferences can also help you decide what to teach in your minilessons. When you're working with students during writing workshop, use a double lens by considering both the individual child and the whole group. As you work with one child or a small group, you might realize that what you're teaching in the conference might benefit the rest of your students. If that's the case, turn it into a minilesson.

You will make many teaching decisions as you confer, but you will also make decisions later when you refer back to your anecdotal records. Whether you are creating lessons based on the writing you gathered from the group or the notes gathered from kidwatching or conferring, you will want to look across your records and use them to help you create minilessons. You can search through the piles of writing you assessed and seek out common needs among the group. You can look across your conferring and kidwatching notes to discover common needs and patterns in your instruction. Studying anecdotal records will help you teach responsively and choose the most timely and impactful lessons.

> **"**
>
> Good writing teachers assess student writers *every day*. One of the most important things, if not *the* most important thing, that defines good writing teachers is that they are constantly learning about their students as writers.
>
> **Carl Anderson (2005)**

As you work with one child or a small group, you might realize that what you're teaching in the conference might benefit the rest of your students. If that's the case, turn it into a minilesson.

References

Alexander, Kwame. (@kwamealexander). 2018. "A kid asked me 'What are some of your techniques for brainstorming?' I answered: Butt. In. Chair. Also, I like to throw ideas around with my writing . . ." Twitter, July 2, 2018. https://twitter.com/kwamealexander /status/1013862095388053504.

Allen, Jennifer. 2006. *Becoming a Literacy Leader*. Portsmouth, NH: Stenhouse.

Anderson, Carl. 2000. *How's It Going?* Portsmouth, NH: Heinemann.

———. 2005. *Assessing Writers*. Portsmouth, NH: Heinemann.

———. 2009. *Strategic Writing Conferences: Smart Conversations that Move Young Writers Forward*. Portsmouth, NH: Heinemann.

Atwell, Nancie. 1998. *In the Middle: New Understandings About Writing, Reading, and Learning*. Portsmouth, NH: Heinemann.

Bergmann, Jonathan, and Aaron Sams. 2012. *Flip Your Classroom: Reaching Every Student in Every Class Every Day*. Eugene, OR: International Society for Technology in Education.

Bomer, Katherine, and Corinne Arens. 2020. *A Teacher's Guide to Writing Workshop Essentials: Time, Choice, Response*. Portsmouth, NH: Heinemann.

Bomer, Randy. 1998. "Transactional Heat and Light: More Explicit Literacy Learning." *Language Arts* 76 (1): 11–18.

Calkins, Lucy. 1994. *The Art of Teaching Writing*. Portsmouth, NH: Heinemann.

Calkins, Lucy, and colleagues. 2013. *Writing Pathways: Performance Assessments and Writing Progressions, K–8*. Portsmouth, NH: Heinemann.

Cornwall, Gaia. 2020. *Jabari Jumps*. Somerville, MA: Candlewick.

de la Peña, Matt. 2015. *Last Stop on Market Street*. New York: G.P. Putnam's Sons Books for Young Readers.

Dyson, Anne Haas, and Celia Genishi. 1994. *The Need for Story: Cultural Diversity in Classroom and Community*. Urbana, IL: National Council of Teachers of English.

Eickholdt, Lisa. 2015. *Learning from Classmates: Using Students' Writing as Mentor Texts*. Portsmouth, NH: Heinemann.

Fletcher, Ralph. 2003. *A Writer's Notebook: Unlocking the Writer Within You*. St. Louis, MO: Turtleback Books.

Goldberg, Natalie. 1986. *Writing Down the Bones: Freeing the Writer Within*. Boulder, CO: Shambhala Publications.

Graves, Donald. n.d. "Answering Your Questions About Teaching Writing: An Interview with Donald H. Graves." https://www.scholastic.com/teachers/articles/teaching-content/answering-your-questions-about-teaching-writing-talk-donald-h-graves.

———. 1983. *Writing: Teachers and Children at Work*. Portsmouth, NH: Heinemann.

Guo, Philip, Joho Kim, and Rob Rubin. 2013. "How Video Production Affects Student Engagement." http://up.csail.mit.edu/other-pubs/las2014-pguo-engagement.pdf.

Hammond, Zaretta. 2014. *Culturally Responsive Teaching and the Brain*. Thousand Oaks, CA: Corwin.

Heard, Georgia. 1999. *Awakening the Heart: Exploring Poetry in Elementary and Middle School*. Portsmouth, NH: Heinemann.

Hechinger Report. 2017. "Kids Asked to Learn in Ways That Exceed Attention Spans." www.usnews.com/news/national-news/articles/2017-12-04/teachers-often-ask-kids-to-learn-in-ways-that-exceed-adult-sized-attention-spans-study-finds.

Hoyt, Alex. 2011. "First Drafts: Gary Soto's 'Talking to Myself' and 'Sunday Without Clouds.'" *The Atlantic*. www.theatlantic.com/entertainment/archive/2011/06/first-drafts-gary-sotos-talking-to-myself-and-sunday-without-clouds/241077.

Hunter, Madeline. 1982. *Mastery Teaching*. Thousand Oaks, CA: Corwin.

Hunter, Robin, and Madeline C. Hunter. 2004. *Madeline Hunter's Mastery Teaching: Increasing Instructional Effectiveness in Elementary and Secondary Schools*. Thousand Oaks, CA: Corwin.

Jensen, Eric. 2005. *Teaching with the Brain in Mind*. Alexandria, VA: ASCD.

Johansen, Dana, and Sonja Cherry-Paul. 2016. *Flip Your Writing Workshop: A Blended Learning Approach*. Portsmouth, NH: Heinemann.

Johnston, Peter. 2004. *Choice Words: How Our Language Affects Children's Learning*. Portsmouth, NH: Stenhouse.

Keats, Ezra Jack. 1998. *Peter's Chair*. London: Puffin Books.

King, Stephen. 2000. *On Writing: A Memoir of the Craft*. London: Hodder & Stoughton.

Krashen, Stephen. 1982. *Principles and Practice in Second Language Acquisition*. Hayward, CA: Alemany Press.

Lamott, Anne. 1995. *Bird by Bird: Some Instructions on Writing and Life*. New York: Pantheon Books.

Le Guin, Ursula K. 1998. *Steering the Craft: Exercises and Discussions on Story Writing for the Lone Navigator or the Mutinous Crew*. Portland, OR: Eighth Mountain Press.

Linder, Rozlyn. 2016. *The Big Book of Details: 46 Moves for Teaching Writers to Elaborate*. Portsmouth, NH: Heinemann.

Mosley, Walter. 2007. *This Year You Write Your Novel*. New York: Little Brown and Company.

Murray, Donald. 2003. *A Writer Teaches Writing*. Belmont, CA: Wadsworth Publishing.

———. 2009. *The Essential Don Murray: Lessons from America's Greatest Writing Teacher*. Portsmouth, NH: Heinemann.

NBC Learn: Writers Speak to Kids. The Learning Forum. www.nieonline.com/thelearningforum/2012writers.cfm.

Nieto, Sonia. 2013. *Finding Joy in Teaching Students of Diverse Backgrounds*. Portsmouth, NH: Heinemann.

Nordquist, Richard. 2019. "12 Writers Discuss Writing." ThoughtCo. www.thoughtco.com/writers-on-writing-1692856.

Owocki, Gretchen, and Yetta Goodman. 2002. *Kidwatching: Documenting Children's Literacy Development*. Portsmouth, NH: Heinemann.

Oxenhorn, Abby, and Lucy Calkins. 2003. *Small Moments: Personal Narrative Writing*. Portsmouth, NH: Heinemann.

Portalupi, JoAnn, and Ralph Fletcher. 2001. *Nonfiction Craft Lessons: Teaching Informational Writing K–8*. Portsmouth, NH: Stenhouse.

Ray, Katie Wood. 1999. *Wondrous Words: Writing and Writers in the Elementary Classroom*. Urbana, IL: National Council of Teachers of English.

———. 2006. *Study Driven: A Framework for Planning Units of Study in the Writing Workshop.* Portsmouth, NH: Heinemann.

UShistory.org. "The Declaration of Independence." www.ushistory.org/declaration/document/rough.html.

Vitale-Reilly, Patricia. 2015. *Engaging Every Learner: Classroom Principles, Strategies, and Tools.* Portsmouth, NH: Heinemann.

———. 2017. *Supporting Struggling Learners: 50 Instructional Moves for the Classroom Teacher.* Portsmouth, NH: Heinemann.

Watson, Renee, and Jason Reynolds. 2017. Interview at the Langston Hughes House, May 28. www.youtube.com /watch?v=GomlBEt6Zm8.

Zinsser, William. 1976. *On Writing Well: An Informal Guide to Writing Nonfiction.* New York: Harper Collins.

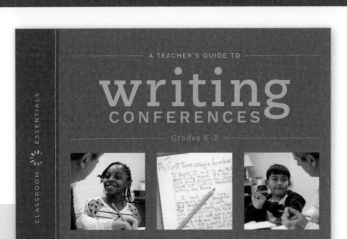

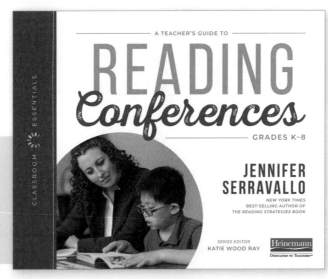

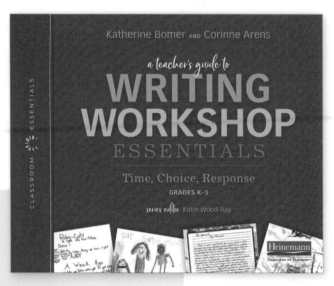

A Teacher's Guide to Writing Workshop Essentials

by Katherine Bomer and Corinne Arens

Grades K–5 / 978-0-325-09972-9
136pp / $21.00

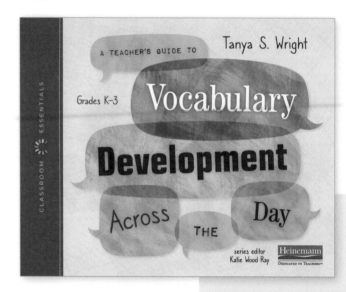

A Teacher's Guide to Vocabulary Development Across the Day

by Tanya S. Wright

Grades K–3 / 978-0-325-11277-0
136pp / $21.00

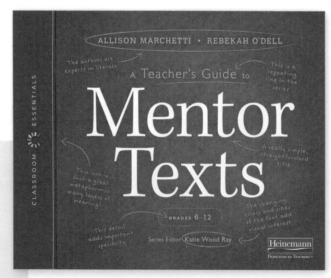

A Teacher's Guide to Mentor Texts

by Allison Marchetti and Rebekah O'Dell

Grades 6–12 / 978-0-325-12003-4
136pp / $21.00